CHICSAVAGES

JOHN FAIRCHILD

SIMON AND SCHUSTER

New York   London   Toronto   Sydney   Tokyo

Simon and Schuster
Simon & Schuster Building
Rockefeller Center
1230 Avenue of the Americas
New York, New York 10020

Copyright © 1989 by John Fairchild

Designed by Karolina Harris
Pictures researched and edited by Vincent Virga
All photographs not specifically credited are courtesy of
Women's Wear Daily/W magazine/M magazine
Manufactured in the United States of America

10   9   8   7   6   5   4   3   2   1

Library of Congress Cataloging in Publication Data
Fairchild, John.
   Chic savages / by John Fairchild.
      p.   cm.
   1. Costume designers—Social life and customs.   2. Fashion.
I. Title.
TT507.F25   1989   89-37136
746.9'2'0922—dc20   CIP
ISBN 0-671-68334-9

For Jill
and to everyone at WWD/W . . .
also a big thanks to the women who helped me:
    Gloria, Gwen, Fran, and Tish
and to Mort Sheinman, who read an early draft
also Vincent Virga, who did the picture research and layout
and to Jeanne Bernkopf, who put the pieces together . . .
Many, many thanks.

CONTENTS

CHIC SAVAGES

1
BABY SAVAGE

I am enclosed securely in a seventeenth-century court-yard in Provence. Leaves whisper across the old stones, and a yellow finch darts from beneath the stone eaves onto a neighboring olive tree, cocks its head, and looks at me quizzically. The fountain plays over the water lilies blooming in an old trough; New Dawn roses climb to the tiled roof of my hideaway. Their scent, mixed with rosemary and thyme, fills the warm air. The days pass quickly here, and I find myself wondering if my world—that of the Chic Savages—exists at all, so far removed does it seem from that of my little finch.

For however improbable it may be—I was born in Newark (how "out" can you get?) and given a straitlaced education (Episcopalian Kent School and Presbyterian Princeton)—that is my world. I know them well, the rich, the famous and the infamous, the power brokers and the powerful, the "Walkers" and the "pushers," the fashionable and the unfashionable; and how they got where they are, and what happens to them once they are there, have always fascinated me.

My association with this savage world began in Paris—then, as now, the nursery of fashion—in the guise of a summer job. I was still at Princeton, but knew my future was involved with the family enterprise, Fairchild Publications.

My family was a very traditional one. My grandfather, E. W. Fairchild, had bought a piece of a Chicago clothing-trade paper in 1890, and over the years he and his brother, L. E., had founded a group of trade publications covering subjects that now range from electronics to fashion, including *Women's Wear Daily,* which we like to think of as required reading for those who design, make, or sell clothes for the American woman, but which *Time* magazine prefers to call "that gossipy, bitchy newspaper of manners, friends and scandal."

An overstatement, surely. I had learned early on that the world of fashion was a gossipy, theatrical, unscrupulous, dogmatic, and opinionated business, and that to succeed, *WWD* had better be alive in this alive business, controversial in this controversial business, smart and snobby in this smart and snobby business. As a result, it approached its world like a tiger and not like a cat.

From all reports, my grandfather was a terribly hard worker. My father always used to tell me that even on Christmas Day my grandfather would come to the office and eat just an orange for lunch. He was always in the office on Sunday, and my father followed in the same tradition. I did not. The truth of the matter is that I was lucky. I inherited an opportunity and tried to take advantage of it.

When I was thirteen, I was sent to Washington to work at a summer job, running errands between the Fairchild office, which was in the Union Bank Building, and the War Production Board.

In subsequent summers, I tried out being a copy boy in the New York office, worked as a reporter and in the Circulation Department, and in between, to complete my training career, I learned what the retail store business was about by joining the training squad of the J. L. Hudson Company in Detroit, at that time the largest department store in the country. I ended up working in Sportswear, where my main job was to make sure that Hudson's always had enough of the paper panties that women used when trying on bathing suits.

In the summer of 1949—I was about twenty and between my junior and senior years at Princeton—I was shipped to the Paris office, 39 rue Cambon, at the top of the Chase Bank Building and across from the Ritz Hotel, to work with B. J. Perkins, my old boss from Washington. Basically, I was there to learn French and to learn about the fashion business, for my father was convinced that the key to our business was fashion, because fashion was in everything, from clothes to food to automobiles: that everything we touched was fashion, a rather progressive idea in those days.

I was still running a lot of errands, for Mr. Perkins rarely left the office, except for lunch. "Fairchild," he would yell, "I'm off to the embassy."

It wasn't long before I realized, fledgling reporter that I was, that Mr. Perkins was headed instead for the Hotel Crillon bar, with his press cronies.

One day, after wending his way back from a long lunch at "the embassy," he lurched into his office, slammed his frosted-glass door, and summoned me. "Fairchild, for once make sure your white jacket is clean. Christian Dior is coming to dinner tonight, and you'll be waiting on the table." He never did introduce me to Dior that night, just used me instead of paying for a real waiter.

I didn't notice anything especially unusual about Dior, except that he seemed a bit shy and more interested in the dinner than in the guests.

What do we mean when we talk about fashion, anyway? For the longest time, the French believed only in couture—clothes made to order—and before the '60s, virtually everything was originals. The French were very slow to move into ready-to-wear—they call it *prêt-à-porter*—but the Italians were much quicker at it. (Most of today's best ready-to-wear clothes are made by Italians, even if they're designed by the French. Just as the French cannot dance together, neither can they manufacture clothes, because two Frenchmen will always be doing something different. The creative ideas are there, but they just can't mass-produce them. Curious.)

Even back in my early Paris days, none of the leading designers could support their studios based on couture sales alone, for very, very few women dressed in the couture. Today, of course, there are even fewer. After all, a very simple suit in the couture can easily cost $10,000, though the designers give all sorts of special prices to people they think are important. French women don't go to the couture very much. Couture's biggest customers are American women and people you've probably never heard of: exceedingly rich Arabs and Germans.

Early on, the designers started making their serious money with perfumes and accessories. Coco Chanel, the mother of all fashion—no one has created anything new since—created the fashion formula that still works today. Before World War II, she employed three thousand people who made couture clothes, accessories, and perfumes. After the Wertheimer family bought out Coco Chanel, they built the great empire that today is the envy of every other fashion firm. It was only with those profits—and the hysterical press coverage they bought—that the top designers could ever afford the luxury of making couture clothes for the very rich.

Today the couture process remains essentially unchanged from what it was thirty years ago. A client will go to a salon, where the designer will have her dummy in the back room and measure the dress on that. The client may have three or four fittings altogether.

Overall, it's a pretty inefficient process. A designer basically starts with a piece of canvas. Some may begin with a sketch, but others, like Ungaro, will start with the canvas because they don't draw very well. Ungaro will take a piece of canvas—no colors, nothing—and marry the fabric to the silhouette of the dummy, adding little black rings for the buttons or other such things. That's the way it works; that is what a great designer does.

Most of the really great designers, like Balenciaga and Chanel, knew how to cut on a live model. I saw Chanel at eighty take her scissors, with a model standing in front of her, and cut an armhole, drawing blood. And the model would just stand there, hour after hour.

Some designers still like to use only one girl. For a long time Saint Laurent had an Indian girl named Kyrat, who, he said, had for him the perfect figure. Other designers may talk about getting their inspiration from some ideal woman, but I've always thought that was mainly for publicity. Lacroix made a big splash with his favorite, the first model with gray hair I'd ever seen in the Paris couture.

Sometimes I'm asked whether there are as many top designers today as there were when I started in the business. I would have to say yes but that the top designers of yesterday had more power. Once upon a time, Mr. Dior or Mr.

Balenciaga would decree that everyone should wear something, and everybody did. Today fashion is more individualistic and sophisticated, and the fads are exhausted a great deal faster. My numerous critics notwithstanding, nobody can dictate fashion anymore; it would be like telling people what they can eat.

Paris still gives fashion authority, but today fashion is born on the world's streets: in the East Village, on the King's Road, on the Corso.

When I began in the business, the top designers were generally acknowledged to be Balenciaga and Dior, and a little bit of Jacques Fath. Each had a totally different style, and each was very powerful, but Christian Dior was certainly the most powerful of them all.

Why? Because his timing was perfect.

Right after World War II, Dior realized that people were ripe for some sort of extravagance—extravagance and romance—a change from the tough times. There was all this fabric available, fabric that had been strictly rationed during the war. So Dior produced his famous long skirt with huge reams of fabric, fairly reeking of luxury. It was like having a good steak all of a sudden.

But fabric has always been the key to good fashion. And it never seems to come from America but usually from France and Italy—today mostly from Italy. Unfortunately, it's becoming harder and harder to obtain, because the best mills don't want to make a fabric for only fifty dresses, while the couturiers insist that if a woman buys a dress for $20,000 she doesn't want to see the same fabric in ready-to-wear. Which is a real problem, and one that is only likely to get worse.

These days, when we at *WWD* cover a couture collection, we try to go and talk to the designer in his studio while he is actually creating the collection, perhaps a month, two weeks, or maybe just three or four days before the opening. We insist on being the only journalists there, and we will photograph ahead of time, even when the seams are not sewed up. Sometimes we shoot so close to our deadline that we have to airbrush the seams closed.

If all this sounds something like a free-for-all, that's because it is. For the designers themselves don't know what is going to sell, what's going to be influential, and neither do we. As Dr. Freud said, nobody knows what a woman wants—and not just women with a lot of money. But it's that mystery that I love most about the business.

Whatever you have heard to the contrary, it's a true crap game, and even the top designers can only basically do what they believe in. Each one sits in a room—four walls, the lights on—with lots of fabric lined up against the wall. They're sketching away—or an Ungaro is fitting on a dummy—and each one is saying to himself, "Now, what am I going to make which is pleasing to me that will also be pleasing to women?"

And this happens four times a year!

These poor designers are also saying to themselves, "I can't make something that's too radical, because then the women who bought the clothes that I made before will get irritated and won't buy my new things. I've got to be careful to *evolve*."

Because there's nothing very new that can come out of fashion. They can change the silhouette, can give the woman broad shoulders or soft ones, no waist or a high waist, a belted dress or a nonbelted dress, a long or a short skirt or can put her in pants, can give her a man's jacket, or can work with the blouse, the hat, the colors, and the buttons—but they're still limited by the anatomy in front of them.

So what's a designer to do? If he's smart, he takes a trip. To New York or to Russia or to India. And like a sponge, he absorbs everything around him, soaking up ideas.

· · ·

Before moving on to introduce you to the savage world of society, which, literally, consumes the fruit of fashion's loom, let me say something about *WWD*'s part in it.

From its early days, *WWD* developed a reputation as the most feared and disliked player in fashion publishing, accused of a string of personality assassinations, cutting insults, and crushing put-downs. Not so. The real issue is that in the fashion business, it's almost against the law to tell the truth, and anyone who steps behind the silk curtain to show how raw the business really is can expect a rough time.

It's not a seamy world, really, but it does seethe with double deals and political ploys, and if you tell the truth about it, report fairly on the scene and refuse to bow down and rave about the hype, you're automatically branded a controversial bastard. Designers go to grotesque lengths to exaggerate their concepts to the press. And the press is just as guilty when it swallows the bait and spews forth huge headlines. The self-importance of our profession is appalling. Otherwise sane editors vie for the "right" seats at every opening and get so worked up over a collection that they practically froth at the mouth. You'd think their work was the only deterrent to the hydrogen bomb.

On the whole, I think the fashion press's power—and *WWD*'s in particular—is greatly overrated. We don't "make" or "break" a designer. Any designer who is good gets ahead. We write what the buyers are saying. Once we headlined a Givenchy collection "Givenchy Is Flop Art," because it *was*. We have been accused of touting Saint Laurent only to taunt Balenciaga and Givenchy. In actuality, the mood of fashion had switched from the elegant monkdom these men exemplified to the fresh visions of Courrèges and Saint Laurent.

Granted, if we learn that Mr. X is about to be fired, we run the story immediately. We realize that the poor man may read about his demise in the paper before his boss has had a chance to tell him, but we can't coddle our subjects, and our personal feelings really don't count.

And as to who has the right to determine who is, or isn't, "best dressed," the answer is no one. The Best-Dressed List is a gimmick and a bunch of rot. All it is good for is the fashion business. Those who are really well dressed want to mind their own business and stay at home. True, those who are dying to make it love being spotlighted, probably because they can tell their husbands it was worth all the money they spent.

When I think of fashion, I conjure up a lot more than body covering. Good fashion is simple. Bad fashion is when a woman exaggerates. Take the period of the big, tight sweaters—Marilyn Monroe stuff. It looked great on Marilyn, but it was grotesque to wear to lunch at a thick-carpeted midtown restaurant. In fact, when a woman walks into a room, I rarely look first at the clothes. I regard the face, sense the mood, the change in the atmosphere. Only then do I look at the dress, which, if it's right for her, flatters and enhances all the rest. I can't stand fashion victims, but true style is something else again. If a woman feels comfortable in her own skin, and then in her clothes, she'll be fine.

What a joy is a woman, young or old, who is dressed not to be "fashiony" but to enhance her normal charm. Some of the women considered by the "experts" to be well dressed are just Barbie dolls. They are plastic. Many of those women we see photographed over and over again have fallen victim to a clumsy hairdresser or to badly designed dresses. There is still nothing like a good sweater and a well-cut skirt or pair of pants.

I see women walking on the street every day who are superbly in fashion without having carloads of money. They have style, which doesn't necessarily mean they look "right" or even that they look "great." One of the covers of another of our magazines, *M,* is tacked to the wall of my office in New York. It pictures a man picking grapes in Burgundy. He is wearing blue coveralls with a blue-and-white-checked shirt, and I doubt very much that he even thought about what he was wearing the day he had his picture taken. He doesn't have to worry about fashion, because he has *style.*

Americans—and possibly even more Europeans—are endlessly fascinated with the cowboy. Now, real cowboys are usually the ones without any teeth, but the cowboy ideal, the Marlboro Man, projects an instinctive style that sets him apart from the rest of the herd. He does it, not by being tasteful—I hate the word "taste"—but by going against the grain, by not following fashion's crowd.

Recently, my wife and I had two English ladies arrive at our house in the South of France. One was wearing a little rose-printed dress with a big hat, and the other some sort of gardening dress, but they had more sheer *style* than another guest who was wearing a brand-new Saint Laurent. They were timeless and full of character. Had they been more "fashionable," they would have been decidedly less stylish.

Am I being too harsh? No, I'm only feeding the hand that bites me, for the fashion business gives every bit as much as it gets from *WWD.* Even I, surely to be numbered among the gentlest of men, have been accused of all manner of excess, and always over issues of fashion, not of style. At one time, there used to be talk in Paris that I was having orgies with animals. And all because of an unfavorable review! Actually, I've only been propositioned once in my life by a male designer, so I must not be very attractive to the breed. But even so, how do these things start?

Take *l'affaire* Trigère. One morning I woke up to find this American designer's advertisement in *The New York Times:* "Dear John, After all these years and so many terrific collections—is it really over between us? You don't call. You don't write. I still love you. Pauline." I've never seen a Pauline Trigère collection and I have certainly never criticized her.

I don't think there is any question that we make fashion judgments at *WWD*. And sometimes we have been wrong. But I can only think that the one-sided snits are simply an easy way for the disgruntled to glean free publicity at the expense of the guileless gruntled.

Yet I know how they feel, because believe it or not, ours is not an easy role. Sometimes I feel like a little boy who spots something enticing and reaches for it, only to have the lid of the jam pot snap upon his finger. Then, of course, I scream like a sixty-two-year-old spoiled brat, but still, I cannot resist putting my finger in the jam pot.

When I hear that Stavros Niarchos, one of the richest men in the world, takes time out of his busy life to kick one of our photographers, I cannot resist writing about it. And when Frank Sinatra, knowing that we've written something about him that he doesn't like, refuses to attend a charity event if *WWD* attends, my joy knows few bounds.

So join me in my world of fun, intrigue, humor, war, and peace—a world that frequently fails to thrill me, often terrifies but never bores me. A world where the appearance of a new designer and a new recipe for chicken pot pie are treated with commensurate jubilation. Together we will search out style, whether we agree about it or not, and stalk the Chic Savages in their well-appointed lairs, even to their very limousines, with windows so shaded that high noon comes and goes without a trace.

In short, come join the dance; and for a change, let the piper pay.

2

WELCOME
TO THE CIRCUS

The fashion circus has three rings: Milan, Paris, and New York. There are sideshows in London, but it is in those three cities that trends are born and die.

Like locusts, thousands of buyers and thousands of press wing their way twice a year to feast, first, on the trends of Milan. They come from as far away as Australia. Recently, they've even come from China and Russia. Behind the dreary walls of Milan there is a world of fashion humming with hard work, and in the end, the city produces some of the world's best clothes.

Come with me, then, to watch the beginning of the fashion parade in Milan.

We are on the plane, flying through the fog, and below us are the farms that surround Milan. If you are smart, you will not have checked your luggage, for at Milan's airport you can wait at least an hour to retrieve it. And your bag may well end up on the carousel carrying the luggage of an SAS flight from Stockholm.

We jump into a little yellow cab and at great speed race into a traffic jam, all the cars bound for Milan, a dreary city if ever there was one. The Milanese manage to escape it regularly on the weekends.

But behind the gray buildings, a lot is going on in business and fashion, for Milan is the fashion capital of Italy and one of the fashion capitals of the world. The weather may be dreary, but the Milanese are not. They love to work and make money, and they are waiting right now to take *our* money—and money from the Germans, the Chinese, the English, and even the French. For the Milanese know how to cut cloth and cut a deal at the same time.

In the unimposing Hotel Gallia, surrounded by the debris of nearby subway construction, the lobby already swarms with buyers and members of the fashion press. The concierge's desk is covered with flowers, bottles of champagne, and boxes of candy—blandishments proffered by the Italian designers and manufacturers to the buyer locusts who have just hit town. Telephones ring constantly as the concierges try to arrange dinner reservations at the In restaurants, which are no longer accepting reservations.

The fight begins.

Will Bergdorf be able to keep the Fendi fur collections exclusively? No. Bergdorf finally decided to drop their $2 million fur department. Still among the Fendis' big customers are the cardinals in the Vatican.

Will Bloomingdale's be able to make peace with Krizia, Italy's leading high-fashion sweater firm?

Will Armani let *Harper's Bazaar* see his collection at the first show? (The second show is for the second-rate press —German and leftover Italian journalists.)

How are the prices? They're always up in Milan. Which has Armani invited to dinner first, Bergdorf Goodman's president or Bloomingdale's president? Or have they been invited at all? Will *Vogue* give its party for a thousand people this season? Is Bice still the restaurant to be seen in, and can you get a reservation?

In the Gallia dining room, I am almost turned away from the door because it's too late for breakfast. There is no room service today; the waiters are on strike against the manager. They just don't like him, according to Alberto, my driver. While I go to get the last two slices of pineapple at the breakfast buffet, someone steals my knife and fork. Where's my coffee?

I want a shower after the long trip. My key card has expired and won't unlock the door, so it must be reinstated. Now I really need a shower. No hot water! My desk is covered with invitations neatly separated with rubber bands for each day. The smell of fruit rotting in cellophane-covered baskets fills the room. I open the window. Below, the small park is littered with papers, and in the slight drizzle the Milanese are on their way to work, rushing. The doorman is trying to stop the limousines and private cars from parking on the sidewalks. They park anyway. Milanese often drive on the sidewalks to pass other cars.

Quickly I close the windows. They are double glass, but I can hear the clanging of the trolley cars as their wheels screech along the steel rails. Even with all the noise in the hallway, I can hear the chambermaid screaming, "Gino, Gino, Gino." Poor thing: I don't think she realizes that Gino is on strike today, and he won't be there, but then tomorrow she might go on strike—so they will have to wait to see each other.

Grasping Monday's invitation, I race down the wide marble staircase to the lobby, past the big plastic plants, and into the limousine, for the dash to the fifty-acre Milan fairgrounds, where in specially constructed tents I will sit together with two thousand other members of the fashion pack.

On the way in, it seems for a moment that we have stumbled onto a Texas cow auction. The roar of the fashion herd, waving invitations in the air and shoving toward the barricades, is deafening. But this hysteria is part of the fashion game, part of the tradition of fashion rudeness. The idea is to keep the buyers and the press waiting in anticipation of the great show about to take place.

The photographers push through their own barricade. They are the first in. They always are. And though they are placed in the pit around the runway, they will stand on their camera cases to get a better view.

On our side, buyers who are normally fierce competitors are suddenly trapped close together inside a narrow passage. The press from all over the world tumble over one another, more than slightly bedraggled from jet lag. *Vogue*'s Grace Mirabella looks as if she might be the headmistress of a New Jersey private school; Carrie Donovan from *The New York Times* clasps her large glasses as a photographer shoves his camera against her head; *Harper's Bazaar*'s June Weir talks with her hands to her publisher, Tony Mazzola, who clutches his raincoat and looks half asleep.

Once past the barricades, it's up the stairs and through strips of plastic curtain that slap you in the face as you finally enter the big tent, where young Italian ushers dressed in blue blazers with brass buttons, red neckties, and American loafers try their best to seat the swaying mob.

Editors and buyers try to pass to their assigned seats along the narrow aisles. All are eager to see what the pecking order for the season will be. Will *WWD* have its honored seat? Will *Vogue* sit closer to the end of the aisle than

Harper's Bazaar? The answer is yes. Will Anna Piaggi, editor of the Italian fashion magazine *L'Espresso,* wear her bird hat with feathers this season, and will she curl her hair over or under her ears? The pack waiting for the show to begin spends the time staring and gossiping.

Cable News Network's Elsa Klensch, her Australian accent rising above the ambient cackle, summons one of the ushers and demands that the photographer in front of her be removed. He stays, crouched against her knees, and when the lights finally go out he rises and blocks her view.

Applause—the show is about to begin. The lights go on again and then off. In the darkness, strange creatures in black can be seen slipping quietly down the runway. The music blares, deafening hard rock, and smoke covers the runway. Models in red run through the smoke. Then klieg lights, hundreds of them, suspended from steel rods, blaze, and an army of models goes down the runway—twirling, glaring, rarely smiling, displaying their superiority and defiance in every body movement. They are like snakes, slipping through the underbrush, raising their heads and flicking their tongues for a second, before moving back into their personal underworld.

These are models who, when challenged, can throw their hips off center or step aside in a way calculated to steal the show. The best of them earn more than $2,000 a show. But for it they walk twenty miles a day, after each show moving on to yet another, where their hair will be pulled and teased, their faces painted with yet more makeup, their bodies twisted and tortured into clothes that no one else could wear and then pushed out onto a new runway for two minutes. They return backstage with aching feet—the shoes rarely fit—to have the dresser rip the clothes off, leaving them shivering and naked, only to have other dresses pulled over their heads in seconds, hair combed, makeup checked, and then it's off again to the runway.

They are soldiers of fortune who never seem to complain,

and at the finale, they float down the runway applauding their master—tonight Gianfranco Ferré—who lifts his glasses to wipe away the tears.

The fight to get backstage after the show to congratulate Ferré begins with *Vogue*'s Polly Mellen, who rises from her chair as she applauds, holding her hands high in the air so that all can see and hear her approval of the collection. Pushing their way, the top store buyers and the press squeeze tightly together, climbing up on the runway, running to be the first to bow to Master Ferré, who, with his jacket off now, is wiping his brow, blowing his nose, still crying. He is surrounded by his court, who spot the important people and make sure they are guided to Ferré.

Some of the Italian press—those devoted to the Ferré camp and not the Versace or Armani camp—are crying too. Fashion hysteria mixes with fashion rudeness as Ferré is covered with all colors of lipstick. He holds one Italian journalist's hands as he looks over his shoulder to see who has come backstage to praise the collection and who has stayed behind.

In the middle of the orgy, the models slump over their chairs; some lie on the floor. They wipe off their makeup, comb their hair, climb into their jeans, and leave through small doors, civilians once again.

Back at the Gallia's Baboon Bar, the buyers gather, ready to give their opinions on the Ferré collection. The remarks are ambiguous. "Good Ferré, but unwearable." "Bad Ferré, not enough newness." "Too much like last season." "We'll wait to see what Armani does before we buy anything." And: "Ferré's a genius, but his clothes can only be worn by tall women, and there aren't enough of them."

I find it hard to believe the buyers, because they are committed in so many ways. How can a store damn a Ferré collection when they have a boutique agreement for several years? How can they criticize when they are trying to unload all of last season's markdowns? So if they do criticize the collection, the next day they may call me and say, "Oh, the Ferré was much better than we thought when we tried his clothes on." Fortunately, Ferré rarely does a bad collection. But his clothes are hard to sell because they are almost as expensive for ready-to-wear as are Paris couture originals. (Even though he has become the chief designer for Dior, he still designs his own ready-to-wear collection.)

The next morning, after a night spent eating their way through the great restaurants of Milan, the fashion pack rises early, yesterday forgotten, and returns to the tent for seven more shows. But in truth, their minds are on Armani, who never shows in a circus tent but only in his small theater, reserved for the fashion press élite and the top buyers. An invitation to Armani's evening show is the most sought-after honor of the Milan fashion scene. What Armani shows is copied by all the other Milanese designers, except for Ferré, who goes his own way.

Armani, who has been called the Monk of Fashion, lives behind the guarded walls of his palazzo on Via Borgonuovo, where he creates, stages his shows, and conducts his $350 million business, all under one roof.

Inside his palazzo, in his penthouse living quarters, there is not one picture on the wall, and only a few rugs in the large sitting areas fitted with gray-beige banquettes abutting gray walls.

The man who revolutionized men's fashions invariably appears in a crewneck navy sweater, simple slacks, and elegant English shoes. And even when Armani entertains, he sits on the floor after dinner, eating chocolates as he strokes his cats. His friends are his staff, and he treats them as family—gently, most of the time, except when he disciplines them, which is often. He is a man of perfection, a man who looks at details as part of the whole. Like Chanel, he can spend hours fitting a collar, mounting a sleeve, choosing a fabric, showing a model how to walk.

He also has a mania for neatness. Upstairs, his personal

wardrobe is systematically arranged, so that all he has to do is to push a button and out will come suits, ties, and shirts—none of which he wears except when he has to leave the monastery for a public appearance. Should Armani encounter Versace, Valentino, or another Italian designer, he avoids contact, if possible; he isn't rude, simply shy and fiercely competitive in everything he does. He knows that an Armani is good and that the rest of fashion copies him mercilessly. He has worked hard to be at the top, and he intends to stay there, the envy of the rest of the fashion business.

Not surprisingly, his collection is the most lavishly praised in the entire hectic week of fashion's nonstop celebration.

In one sense, the Italians have won the battle of fashion. Today they produce clothes for every country, including France. Many of the top French designer labels—including Ungaro, Dior, Lacroix, Rykiel, Montana, and Gaultier—appear on clothes that are manufactured in Italy. It was just after the war that the Italians slowly began their invasion of France, and today even the French have to admit that they are dependent on the Italians for some of the best design ideas. (The Germans might be the largest exporters of ready-to-wear in the world, but so far they have failed to capture the high-fashion market.) The Italian fashion monopoly is even more complete because in addition to clothes, the Italians are responsible for designing and producing some of the most beautiful fabrics in the world. Where Lyons, France, was once the capital of silk, Como has taken over. Italian woolens are dominant on the high-fashion scene.

Romeo Gigli, who claims to be an Italian aristocrat, invaded Paris from his base in Milan with a startling fashion bang in March 1988. His oversize bag-lady clothes, inspired by Japanese designers, made him the star of the season, the man of the fashion moment. He was on the cover of *W* with a gold lamé coat ($37,000 price tag if ever delivered), and *Mirabella,* Murdoch's new fashion magazine, gave him six pages. But staying power is the name of the game for Gigli and for fashion magazines. We will see. Anyway, Caroline of Monaco started wearing Gigli, and other Milanese designers watched with envy the Gigli success.

The Italian invasion of Paris continues. In January 1989, Valentino trunked his couture show to Paris from Rome, killing off what is left of Rome couture. Even the leader of Italian fashion, Giorgio Armani, showed his collection at a big charity event in Paris.

The big rush to Europe—to Italy and then to France (with a brief stop in England)—leaves American fashion way out in the cold and gives American designers an inferiority complex. They shouldn't feel inferior about their fashion, but Americans do because they are up against a Seventh Avenue mentality and an antiquated manufacturing system that really doesn't give them a chance to be more creative. First of all, they cannot get the wonderful workmanship offered to the Europeans. Then they have union problems. They are forced to manufacture the rigid union way, where handwork, sometimes essential to the best in high fashion, is practically nonexistent. I remember Pauline Trigère, who has been around the track a long time, telling me, when shopping her competitors in Palm Beach, that she couldn't believe the low price of a double-faced Valentino coat.

"No way can we compete, pricewise and qualitywise," she said. Yet Americans could make the same coat, with at least the same quality or design talent, if they just had the workmanship. American couture clothes, however, are still not priced competitively with some of the good European imports. One wonders whether the American fashion industry shouldn't look at itself in the mirror and try to figure out how it can do better. To be sure, we have great designers, who sometimes are lacking in inspiration because they do not have access to the finest fabrics. Fabric mills in Italy reserve their best fabrics for a Saint Laurent, an Ungaro, an Armani.

So what we do get from American designers are nicely styled, wearable clothes that are sometimes lacking in fantasy. A Calvin Klein fashion has just enough style to please the American woman. Ralph Lauren, interestingly enough, works in a vacuum of styles from the past—clippings of fashion history. His design staff in the back room pore over fashion documents, searching for some old idea that might look right for today. One has only to look in at his beautiful store in Manhattan to feel the nostalgia.

This should not be construed as criticism of Lauren or Klein. They are probably the best stylists in the world. They have built billion-dollar fashion empires and their styles are not only for Americans but for the rest of the world as well. Lauren's clothes, especially his men's fashions, are international. His style is coveted even by snobbish Europeans.

So what is wrong with the Americans?

Nothing.

It's true that when it comes to creative fashion—ideas that are going to be seen all over the world and be knocked off by other designers—we do not see Americans influencing the Europeans. Yet the all-American concept of easy dressing, or sportswear, has swept the globe.

I have always felt that if American designers were working in Europe, with all the quality and craftsmanship and that indefinable European atmosphere and the European eagerness to be different for novelty's sake, they could be better style leaders than anyone.

Americans have tried working in Europe and have failed. Zack Carr, who was Calvin Klein's assistant, worked in Italy for GFT, probably one of the best manufacturers (of Valentino, Armani, and Ungaro, among others). Carr created a collection, and it bombed. So far, the best Americans have done is to be assistants in the top European fashion houses, but even there they have to give way to the English, who have turned out to be the most sought-after assistants on the European fashion circuit.

Interesting, when you think that except for Vivienne Westwood and Jean Muir, English fashion has remained, for the most part, confined to the British Isles. It doesn't seem to travel well, at least so far.

But what is really frustrating is to see European designers invade our stores and then return home with American sportswear ideas to put into their collections. Armani dispatches a team of young designers to the United States every six months to check out the American scene—including the thrift stores. He pays special attention to California, because he feels that's where the action is. He avoids the East Coast, which he feels is sterile. He especially avoids New York.

European and American designers, then, steal their fashions from everywhere. One of America's most successful designers—and the darling of many a Chic Savage—rarely misses a trick. I have seen Oscar de la Renta spot a beautifully dressed woman at a party and peel the clothes off her back with his eyes.

And the fashion world loves to catch one designer stealing from another. De la Renta sees a front-page sketch of a Saint Laurent dress in *WWD,* and that morning he digs out a sketch from his old collection to show that he beat YSL to the punch. I have seen a gray peplum suit that was designed when Bohan was at Dior form the basis of Oscar's collection after he saw it at a New York wedding. Bohan sees his suit on the front page of *WWD*—credited this time to Oscar— and he only smiles.

The truth is that many designers *like* to be copied. It's all part of the fashion sport. The sad thing, though, is when a designer like Vivienne Westwood sees her ideas appear all over the globe—even in Paris at Christian Lacroix—and never receives any credit.

The game of finding out and telling who copies whom is basically a futile exercise, because everyone copies everyone else. There is no such thing as a truly original idea on the fashion map. Saint Laurent goes to Russia or the Tyrol or Marrakech. He borrows from painters like Braque, Picasso, and Mondrian. Karl Lagerfeld might look at a portrait of Marie Antoinette, Giorgio Armani at a Marlboro ad for the American cowboy. Ralph Lauren might go see an old Cary Grant comedy. Oscar de la Renta will study more than the bride at a wedding. And, of course, every designer pays particular attention to the competition.

When fashion gets out of hand, it is generally true that all designers return to Chanel. She was the forerunner of those few, such as Saint Laurent, Armani, and the late Cristóbal Balenciaga, who have managed to create timeless clothes. With minor changes here and there, a Saint Laurent, an Armani, and the old and new Chanels seem to pass into the category of the eternal wardrobe.

When a designer is copied and when his fashions are worn everywhere and by everyone, then you can say, "That's a real designer, not just a manufacturer of boring body covers." Many clothes are commercially successful, but their look is borrowed: a suit jacket from Armani, a wrapped skirt from Dior, an accessory from Chanel, and the fashion mood—which is so important—from Ungaro. What you wind up with is a fashion soup mixed together with all sorts of fashion vegetables, and the soupmaker makes millions off someone else's creations.

The shape of all fashion begins with the silhouette, but there are only a few designers capable of creating a new silhouette. And it is these designers—the giants—whose moods we follow. We want to know where they go, whom they see, what they are thinking on a daily basis. They are our heroes and, sometimes, our nightmares.

Designers, by their natures, are more than neurotic. They are combinations of movie icons and rock stars, painters, sculptors, and, yes, business people who love money and who love being tycoons.

There are six designers today who are true twinkling stars: Yves Saint Laurent, Giorgio Armani, Emanuel Ungaro, Karl Lagerfeld, Christian Lacroix, and Vivienne Westwood. From them, all fashion hangs by a golden thread. If the thread breaks, if they make a mistake, billions of dollars may be lost. All eyes are on these six: they show the rest of the industry where to go.

Of the six, British Vivienne Westwood is the designer's designer, watched by intellectual and far-out designers, including Jean-Paul Gaultier. She is copied by the avant-garde French and Italian designers, because she is the Alice in Wonderland of fashion, and her clothes are wonderfully mad—fantastic enough to be worn at the Mad Hatter's tea party. Yet, copied as she is, Westwood struggles in her World's End shop in London, living from hand to mouth. What a pity she never did conclude a deal with Armani, who recognized her talent but couldn't manage the fantasy of it all. The last time I saw Vivienne she was dressed more like the Queen in Harris tweeds, but she still wore those high-laced pilgrim shoes.

Incidentally, in all my years with these six designers, I have never heard one of them say: "Look, the rest are only following me." It's not that they are modest; in reality, they have big egos when they stop to think about themselves; they just have too much to do. They feel responsibility weighing daily.

Fashion is something to be enjoyed like a fine meal: you eat it, you digest it, and then you go on to the next meal. Well, the six are busy cooking up fashion meals all year long. They never really get out of the kitchen.

With no holds barred, I would like to go into the world of the six—these giants of fashion who, just like any other creative people, are never really sure of what they are doing. One mark of a great designer is the fact that he is not superconfident about himself. His aim is to please women and to make them feel right: romantic, easy, but joyous when they wear his clothes.

Fashion's aim is to please, and deep in their hearts, these six designers want only to please their customers—to add a little joy to their lives. Because it's a myth that even the richest women in the world—women who can spoil themselves by wearing the most expensive clothes in the world —are truly secure. The fact is that the clothes created by the top designers only help them feel more secure within themselves—secure enough to carry on their ordinary privileged lives.

When a woman walks into a room and a man or another woman tells her she looks great—that's really about all she can ask for at that moment. So maybe the time, the price, and the effort to look great are really not so frivolous after all. We all have to eat, so why not enjoy a good meal, fine wine, a little romance? And why not look great while indulging, even though we know that clothes are just another fantasy in our not-so-wonderful lives?

Looking great and feeling great are not all that bad. I know that self-indulgence is frowned upon these days, but I don't see how anything that gives life a romantic lift and a little joy can be put down as wrong. Being a top designer can be compared to being a medical diagnostician, and if in the end their patients are made to feel better, then great doctors and great designers certainly constitute noble professions. Laugh at that conceit if you will, but fashion diagnoses people's needs. Nothing more. The how is another story.

So there they are, the six, locked up in their studios surrounded by assistants, bolts of fabric, clippings from *WWD, W,* and all the other fashion publications, trying to decide: What should I do this time? Staring from on high is the female form, in all its youthful beauty, or middle-aged charm, or even old age. The same form each season, married to a new idea—not so new as to shock but new enough to tempt a woman to buy. For temptation is the name of the game, because the truth is, women need only a few clothes to survive. Why should they go out and buy more clothes when there are so many other ways to spend money? So fashion must seduce women into buying.

Can the designer transform a woman? Designers have to think so. Can the designer persuade her to change her look without disguising the body, removing her femininity? There are some problems that even the greatest doctor would prefer not to face. There are no miracle drugs, no operations. The body cannot be altered.

Contrary to popular belief, there is no conspiracy to change fashion for the sake of change—no safe house in Geneva where designers plot their new assaults together. In fact, designers have never agreed on any one fashion. Among themselves they rarely agree about anything. Even to persuade designers to show together is a major undertaking, akin to the staging of an Italian opera. After each show, the designers' comments about one another and their works are usually unprintable.

But whether they admit it or not, they are influenced by the six. With so many forces pushing on them, most designers must follow the fashion dictums of these leaders.

The fashion establishment may howl at the six names I have chosen, demand some added, others removed. Everyone in fashion has a strong and even a passionate view of this small, golden, unreal world. Certainly other names could be added to the end of the list. Marc Bohan, until recently the head of design at Christian Dior, and Hubert de Givenchy are both backed by powerful conglomerates and have maintained standards equal to those of the other designers, and they have dressed some of the world's most elegant women.

But their trendmaking abilities have been limited. (Bohan is a trendsetter only with his suits, though he manages to sell more expensive couture clothes than all the other Paris designers except for Saint Laurent.) They are stars in the money-losing business of couture clothes. As a matter of fact, there are now so few private customers left for made-to-order clothes that Saint Laurent has taken to lending evening dresses for a night to the "right women," just so other women, not as elegant but wealthy, will be seduced into buying a Saint Laurent.

The couture business is so rarefied that if in a season Saint Laurent can make and sell five hundred "originals," that is considered a good showing. What Saint Laurent and the other couture designers are really doing is exhibiting expensive museum pieces, which, if purchased at cost, average out to the price of a new Mercedes. A Saint Laurent model can range from $7,000 on up for a simple suit, a daytime dress can cost $5,000, and for evening dresses the prices hit the sky: Ivana Trump paid $37,000 just for a beaded jacket from Christian Lacroix. Yet in spite of such prices, a *maison couture* makes no money at all and in most cases loses on every fitting for a customer.

The Paris couture is endangered. There are fewer private customers—practically no French customers who really pay. The weak dollar caused the Americans to disappear. Only a few Italians, Germans, and Arabs keep ordering clothes from the major couture houses. As a result, the couturiers with the big names have had to rely more and more on their perfumes and on licensing everything from clothing to accessories to home furnishings.

At one time, Pierre Cardin put his name on plumbing, Saint Laurent on cigarettes and doormats in Japan. The couture name can still generate an enormous amount of publicity and turn enormous profits at very little expense to the couturier. But when a couture star fades, when a designer's name is overlicensed, the whole business can come crashing down. The smart European designers manage to stash their money in private accounts in Switzerland and elsewhere.

American designers are always asking me how it is that European designers seem to live so much better. Not that the Americans live badly at all. I would guess the Americans just pay their taxes, while some of the Europeans have been clever in setting up their businesses. One French designer has his office in Switzerland, and any licensing deal has to be put through the Swiss office. What goes on in Switzerland doesn't pass as normal in the rest of the business world, where taxes are part of everyday life.

But speaking of money, why do designers go to all the expense of holding on to those workroom tailors, seamstresses, and all the luxuries of a Paris couture house when they know they are probably not going to reproduce their couture models? Because designers claim they need their expensive establishments as laboratories to create in.

Walk into a Paris studio with the DÉFENSE D'ENTRER sign on the door, and there before you, in full light, waits the master of fashion, Yves Saint Laurent, immaculate in his white smock. (Dior and Balenciaga started the tradition of the white smock, and Givenchy carried it to perfection, insisting that his be made in his own atelier.) Saint Laurent sits at a modern tabledesk piled high with multicolored pens and pencils. He sketches on long sheets of a heavy white linen-like paper—one sketch to a sheet. At his feet sleeps his English bulldog, Moujik.

Or there is Emanuel Ungaro in his smock, standing much shorter than the model he is literally pinning up. Ungaro works with a white toile to shape his dresses. The fabric is married to the toile only after the master is satisfied that the new creation is perfect in shape and proportion. For fashion *is* shape and proportion; all the rest—skirt length, shoulder width, sleeves, neckline—are only minor details. The essential step is in molding the toile to the model's perfect body, for every designer must start with the ideal. An ordinary woman is never in the mind of a great designer, at least not in the beginning. It is the memory of that ideal woman that carries him through the season.

The model standing in front of Saint Laurent or Ungaro is a mechanical being, perfect in form, who is not there to speak to her master, let alone offer an opinion. She is paid for standing for hours, while her master rips and cuts and then perhaps starts all over again.

In the atelier of Christian Lacroix, Marie Seznec, his favorite model, enters the room from behind a screen. The staff is silent. Even the pins dropping from her skirt as Lacroix rips away at the hem fall silently. There is only the rustle of taffeta in the room, as Marie glides away from her master, then quickly returns as he beckons by waving two fingers like a conductor. He crouches in front of the runway, then is up quickly, opening the top of the dress, then letting it fall, the white polka dots on a black background drifting to the floor as slowly as snowflakes. The model covers her breasts, while his *première,* the head of the workroom, who used to work with Saint Laurent, kneels at her feet. The master turns to the right, then to the left. He walks away and turns back, his eyes on the model again.

"Walk, walk," he says softly, and the mechanical doll, wearing just the skirt, is off down the runway. Lacroix clasps his hands to his chin and once more crouches at the end of the runway. Marie turns and comes back to her master. Jean-Jacques Picart, the public-relations muse, has been lying on his back, looking at the ceiling. He says nothing but pretends to sleep. Lacroix embraces the skirt, which just for that moment seems to hang by itself, empty. He replaces the top part of the dress, strokes the pouf lovingly, pushing it to her body as if to get rid of it. Now he embraces Marie, kisses her gently on both cheeks, and sends her floating like a puffy cloud back to the plain dressing room. The dream is shattered. That moment of glory, when the master approves of the dress and maybe of the mannequin herself, is over. Everyone is applauding—loudly. Picart is up off the floor. Lacroix has given his blessing to that one dress. And the blessings go on way into the night—for each suit, dress, evening dress, pant, hat, and accessory. Even the shoes must be blessed.

Recently I talked to some Harvard Business School students who were working on a fashion case study. I had a hard time convincing them that the fashion game could not be plotted on a graph—that there was no exact science to fashion. And that in the courses fashion schools offered there was far too much emphasis on merchandising and too little on technique: how to cut a dress, a suit, a coat.

For workmanship is still the key to good clothes, and sadly, today that workmanship is rapidly disappearing. The seamstress and tailor in the Paris couture and in Italy are endangered and could easily disappear, as they have in New York. As one top Seventh Avenue designer told me: "My workroom costs me a fortune—a real fortune. Still, when I examine a Saint Laurent suit costing my client $10,000, I know that my workroom could never in a thousand years and at any price come close to making a suit like that."

Only the Paris couture can afford the luxury of these workrooms, where women sit slumped over on stools sewing away on that one dress destined, they are sure, to make fashion history. I have seen these women applaud with tears in their eyes when their creation appears on the runway—a moment worth all the agony of fashion.

3
THE BOTTOM LINE

After writing their orders and spending millions of dollars in Milan, the fashion locusts take flight for Paris, where they will spend more than fifty percent of their European budgets. Saks and Bloomingdale's, those two great rivals, have photographed all the important collections. All of the stores have pored over even the minutest details, down to every button and seam. Across the world in Hong Kong, copies of the Italian clothes just presented on the runways are being duplicated so that they can be in the stores in a matter of weeks. Other buyers, again drawing on the ideas they have seen in Milan, are designing private-label fashions just stolen off the runway. The fashion jungle is never quiet.

The stores, the manufacturers, and the anonymous quick copiers are racing against each other to turn out the hot numbers for the new season. Big companies like The Limited (1988 net sales of $4,070,777,000), which have successfully taken high fashion from all over the world to small-town America, where there was little fashion to choose from, have ordered, based on news from Milan and later from Paris, yarns in the new colors, the new shapes of sweaters, prints to be produced as far away as Hong Kong and China, and as close as Puerto Rico. In Columbus, Ohio, headquarters of The Limited, the company has built its own airstrip to handle shipments from all over the world. Efficient to the end, The Limited even has its own U.S. customs inspector on the tarmac, to speed the foreign-made fashions to their stores.

Milan and Paris will always be at war, as there is little or no cooperation between the two fashion capitals. Milan, as usual, was first on the runways for the fall showings and Paris set its dates two weeks later, meaning that the stores and the fashion press have to return to the U.S. and then come back again. True to their tradition of being unnecessarily difficult, the French merely shrug their shoulders, self-confident enough to expect the fashion establishment to follow orders.

Are they justified? In a way, yes, but with the dollar weaker and business conditions not the best, they had better be careful. Already they have seen the Italians successfully invade the fashion market, and they have also watched as most high-quality French clothes have begun to be manufactured in Italy. Nevertheless, season after season, the fashion experts—if there are any experts in this business—solemnly declare after the Milan and Paris shows that Paris is still the birthplace of fashion.

To be truthful, the stores are fortunate to have both Paris and Milan, because Italian and French fashion complement each other. In simplest terms, Italy is the fashion capital for everyday sportswear and Paris the place for sophisticated, less "easy" fashions. In the forty years since the Italians entered the lists, after World War II, they have successfully adopted the American idea of real clothes for everyday living and adapted it so that it possesses a more fashiony appeal. In short, the Italians have surpassed American sportswear designers by increasing the fashionability of the clothes.

With most women working today, it would seem that the Italians have the upper hand, but they are limited in their design concept because they don't understand how to change their fashion moods for evening. They tend to the almost vulgar at night. And a designer's environment definitely influences his clothes. The French, snobbish and set in their ways to the end, have remained true to their tradition of a more studied and sophisticated couture—clothes that rely more on cut, color, and shape.

Clearly, there is little that could be called "pure fashion" in this contrary and complicated business. But whatever purity there is, in look and in concept, it is the creation of Yves Saint Laurent, Giorgio Armani, and Emanuel Ungaro. These three, who largely avoid the social scene altogether, are the most influential designers of our time. In their isolation, they create clothes that are modern and daring. Ungaro, sometimes, can be almost too daring, as when, in his most exotic dreams, he turns women into strange birds of paradise. Saint Laurent, on the other hand, rarely goes to extremes—except when he dresses women in Picasso and Braque paintings.

In an effort to grab the headlines from their competitors, sometimes even these two great masters get carried off to the wilder shores of fashion. Even for them, the pitfalls are always there—clothes that are too intellectual, too nouveau riche, too pretentious. Rarely can a designer be too simple in his clothes, but there is always the danger that simplicity can become boring. It's not an easy assignment, trying to please all women. Nevertheless, women of the world have a good sense of what is right for them. They want good taste, but not without some sort of fantasy. And they want change, want to be amused with that something different to add sparkle to their days and nights.

The tug-of-war between the stores and the top designers who fight to have their clothes shown and sold properly is never-ending. Most of the top designers have, in disgust, forsaken the big department stores and the top specialty stores and, instead, have opened boutiques. In some cases, these have been successful, but for the most part the Madison Avenue designer stores are money-losing operations for the designers.

The one exception has been the best boutique in America —and probably in the world—that of Ralph Lauren at Madison Avenue and Seventy-second Street. Lauren is a kind of merchandising genius: there is a distinct, unforgettable Ralph Lauren image—his name represents a certain quality and style. He stands alone as a merchandiser of fashion, not simply with smart and elegant advertising but with a solid concept based on important and great styles from the past. Deep down, he seems to have discovered, most everyone wants to look like a Wasp. Total retail sales that embody this fantasy are close to $2 billion, making Lauren America's richest designer. (He is topped still by Pierre Cardin.)

Ironically, his success stems from his own deep desire to live like a Wasp, a yearning that may stem from his growing up in the Bronx (around the corner from Calvin Klein). He is probably the most personally insecure designer in the business, a man whose real dream is to be a movie star. By his own admission, on nights when he is feeling low and tired, he walks through the empty aisles of his store, admiring "just the look of the place."

He flies in his private jet to his many homes—the old Dillon family house in Round Hill, Jamaica; his two-thousand-square-mile ranch in Colorado, where he lives out his western dream; his Montauk beach home; and, most recently, his manor house in Katonah, New York, where he is creating the most English of English country homes, complete with a full-time British mechanic to serve as "automobile groom." He has hired an ex-butler from Buckingham Palace "to teach the kids table manners," and when young members of the British royal family—not known as big spenders—shop at the Lauren boutique in London, one wonders if Lauren hasn't carried coals to Newcastle.

Still, the British love Lauren's English-American look. As for the designers, Christian Lacroix and Oscar de la Renta have graciously praised Ralph Lauren sportswear in print and happily posed in their Lauren wardrobes.

Interestingly enough, most of the top designers never wear their own men's clothes. Saint Laurent is immaculate in Carenci (Milan), Valentino wears Carenci (Rome), and Bill Blass, Marc Bohan, and Hubert de Givenchy favor Huntsman (London). But I'm sure they have something of Ralph Lauren.

Why not? The man has something special—a proper style in proper taste, with just enough fashion appeal to satisfy. What more can you ask of a designer these days?

Calvin Klein is the other supermerchandiser of his own name, having built a fashion empire with his school pal Barry Schwartz. The three Bronx boys—Lauren, Klein, and Schwartz—grew up in the same neighborhood, where Klein and Schwartz were friends and both knew Lauren. Klein carried his fashion designs in a suitcase directly to the stores, while Lauren showed his neckties. Today the Klein business is worth close to a billion dollars, and, obviously,

Calvin and Barry have dollars to burn. But while Schwartz races and breeds horses and leads a quiet life between the Carlyle and a farm in upstate New York, Klein struggles with personal problems—alcohol, drugs, sex.

The first time I visited Calvin in his West Side apartment —starkly modern, somber and sad, with Georgia O'Keeffe desert paintings, heavy skulls and bones—I felt I could be in a Seventh Avenue showroom or in some gallery in Philadelphia. Lunch was brought in while we photographed his "couture collection," and I remember going to the refrigerator for some ice and finding that the shelves were bare. Obviously, Calvin didn't really live there but only slept there from time to time, high up in his penthouse tower overlooking the park.

In the early days of his career, Calvin spent wild weekends partying on Fire Island, returning Monday on the seaplane, exhausted from the fun, and confiding to friends at lunch, "I have to settle down." His erotic advertisements and his jeans campaign had become world famous. His image—the sexy young designer in the true American spirit, tall, good-looking, impeccably tailored—appeared everywhere. The celebrity of celebrities, he followed in the footsteps of Halston, who had reached the top of the fashion show-biz heap only to come crashing down, the victim of cocaine.

Calvin lopes to his table at The Four Seasons' Bar Room before his guests arrive. The serious businessmen, publishing tycoons, and book editors are all looking at him. He is recognized not because of his advertising campaigns but because he has star quality. He smiles, bows, shakes hands like a handsome politician running for office. Klein orders a Bloody Mary from Julian, the headwaiter, and within minutes, Tom Margittai, the restaurant's co-owner, crosses the room to greet Calvin Klein, Designer, who is just as important as anyone else in the restaurant.

In truth, he is not really Calvin Klein; in his stores and in the world at large, he is known as "Calvin," and thought of still, in his mid-forties, as a charming boy. When you create an image that so enraptures the general public, you come to believe that you are that person—in Calvin's case, the sexy, handsome, and daring young man on the flying trapeze, always ready for a fall.

My colleague Michael Coady and I are sitting opposite Calvin. "I'm in love," he tells us. "Yes, with Kelly," he confirms.

Several weekends before, we had run into Calvin and Kelly on Nantucket; both wore white linen. They were looking for property: "miles of beachfront." We returned to New York with them on their large rented jet—two young lovebirds sipping Dom Pérignon as they zoomed back to Manhattan in the twilight. "I've had enough of the wild life —the late nights out, the drinking, all the fun and games. I'm old enough to settle down."

No sooner had we learned about their pending marriage than Calvin invited us to come after lunch to a private showing of his new collection. "It would make Kelly and me so happy. She's waiting there to see you." His bride-to-be, Kelly Rector, had been working with Calvin as an assistant designer, and when we arrived at 498 Seventh Avenue, we could easily detect Kelly's romantic hand in the new collection.

Calvin removed his jacket and started pacing back and forth with his hand on his hip, going through each coat, suit, dress, skirt, and even the blouses, explaining in minute detail why women would like "everything." The clothes still offered that Klein slickness, perfectly styled and matched in colors and accessories, but when it came to evening wear, Kelly—his new muse—had taken over. Instead of the skirt-sweater look, without any details, Kelly's seductive influence—ruffles, plunging necklines, body fitting: all the marks of a real woman—was there. I caught Kelly smiling at me with her bright, innocently knowing eyes; she had worn the show-stoppers from the collection that night on the jet winging its way back from Nantucket.

Before long they were married in Rome, alone except for Nuno Brandolini and his wife, Melissa, who had worked in the studio with Kelly. The American Embassy and the Agnellis had helped to obtain the license necessary for a foreigner to marry in Rome. Paul Wilmot, Calvin's PR person, had leaked the news to the press, and we had rushed a reporter over for an exclusive interview with the new couple. This was Calvin's second marriage. Prior to her joining Calvin, Kelly, who is one-quarter American Indian, had come out of Ralph Lauren's studio, and Lauren, who never has a bad word for anyone, was delighted with the news. "Kelly was a nice girl," he told me. "And talented too."

After *W* and *Women's Wear Daily* came out, *Vanity Fair* put the Klein couple, both dressed in the best of white, on their cover. André Leon Talley, who had been a fashion editor and head of our Paris office, styled the *VF* cover and wrote an article that made Kelly and Calvin sound like the world's most perfect couple. (Talley, tall and talented, mixed gracefully in the fashion world and in society on both sides of the Atlantic. He hadn't mixed too well with me, though, and one day, without warning, he had marched over to the American Embassy and resigned his post at *W* and *Women's Wear Daily,* declaring in a written statement that I had treated him, a black man, "like a plantation owner would.")

It didn't take long before the Kleins were at all the best New York parties. They rented luxurious houses in Palm Beach and East Hampton, always close to a stable so Kelly could ride. And win ribbons: she's really very good. Calvin bought her horses—the best—and the Duchess of Windsor's jewels at auction. At smart tables all over New York, Kelly Rector Klein would show up with the Duchess's pearls looped around her lovely neck.

They also looked for apartments, but because Calvin was

considered such a "high-profile figure," they were turned down at most of the best addresses despite glowing letters of recommendation from people who felt they should be in a "good building." The boards who run New York's cooperative apartments are reputed to be as narrow-minded as they are stupid, but even so, the gossip columns exploited the news that the Kleins had been rejected—a humiliation that many famous people, including Richard Nixon and Gloria Vanderbilt, have had to endure. In the interim, Kelly lived from time to time in her old apartment and Calvin in his.

But Calvin is tough. Before his marriage to Kelly, there were evil rumors that he was dying of AIDS and that he was in a hospital having transfusions. A designer phoned me to say that a friend had seen Calvin being transported to a hospital in the Midwest to be treated. Then, while I was in Milan, Italian radio announced in a news report from New York that Calvin had died from AIDS, and my phone at the Gallia rang most of the night with inquiries from Paris and New York: was it true? Calvin plowed courageously on, even raising close to a million dollars in one evening at an AIDS benefit at the Javits Convention Center. He moved into that huge hall with Elizabeth Taylor on his arm, and you could feel that the masses gathered for the event—the designers, the show-business types, and the other personalities—were there not so much to see Elizabeth Taylor as to see Calvin back from the dead. A macabre evening, if ever there was one.

At that point, everybody assumed that Calvin's wild days and nights were over, once and for all. But not so. Less than two years into the marriage, Calvin was seen alone at night, partying all over again. Kelly left the business and spent more time riding, while Calvin flew back and forth—in the winters from Palm Beach and in the summers from East Hampton.

Even so, there were no signs of a truly major problem

except, again, for those evil tongues—the gossip columnists —who kept implying that the marriage wasn't exactly made in heaven. A good friend described the scene in Palm Beach: "I went down to their house for a weekend. André Leon Talley and Paul Wilmot were there. We had wonderful food, and for each guest there was a car. Calvin appeared only at meals, but he was on the telephone the rest of the time, talking to his bankers. Big deals were in the works, I guess."

Shortly thereafter, the news came out over the wire— issued by Wilmot, the voice of Klein: Calvin had decided to enter Hazelden in Minnesota for treatment of drug and alcohol abuse. What we didn't know at the time was that one of the scandal sheets already had the story and was about to pop it on the front page, forcing Wilmot to get the news out fast in hope that it would soon be forgotten. Apparently, the fact that a fashion designer was entering a drug treatment clinic was thought to be just as newsworthy as when Betty Ford or Elizabeth Taylor set out to travel that same hard path.

Kelly was scarcely seen by anybody while Calvin was undergoing treatment. The regimen is psychologically severe, Calvin told me later, especially when the Hazelden doctors bring the entire family together to confront the patient with the extent of *their* problem. "Mental surgery," Calvin called it. Then, just as Calvin was being discharged (he was determined to attend his daughter Marci's graduation from Brown) and enthusiastically hooking up with Alcoholics Anonymous, Liz Smith and Billy Norwich of the New York *Daily News* waged public warfare over the state of the Calvin-Kelly marriage.

In fact, while Calvin had been at Hazelden, Kelly—who had a large hand in persuading Calvin to submit to treatment—had moved them both into a Georgian town house on Seventy-sixth Street between Fifth and Madison avenues. In two months she had completely redecorated and made a new home for Calvin, and the day he returned, there she was, standing in the window, half hidden behind the curtain, waiting for him.

Soon Calvin calls me for lunch, and there we are, just like old times, back at The Four Seasons.

"It was hard—very hard," the new Calvin begins. "You see, I thought I was invincible—that I could do anything, overcome everything. Then one morning I just couldn't move, after all the drinking, then more drinking, and then the Valium. For the first time in my life I realized that I was helpless. So I entered Hazelden and stayed a month." With a big smile and that innocent boyish look, he is talking again. "And now I have a new life. I'm enjoying different things, and I'm off the fast track. Kelly and I have a new circle of friends, and last summer I took up riding and sailing and just staying home."

Silence.

"Please, John, don't worry about me; order some wine."

We talk about his show, which is a few weeks away, but he isn't urging me to come and see it in advance, as in the past. "Do your best," I tell him. "There's always another collection next season." Calvin looks reassured and eats his pasta. As we leave the restaurant, he takes my hand firmly and embraces me.

Calvin, in his way, is a creature of the media, but not all fashion images are created with powerful advertising. The dean of American fashion, sixty-seven-year-old Bill Blass—handsome and debonair—has spent a lifetime charming important clients, including the Nancys—Reagan and Kissinger—Judy Peabody, Casey Ribicoff, first lady Barbara Bush, and Pat Buckley, among others.

Like many Midwesterners who are creative and spirited, Bill had picked up stakes and left his mother and sister in Fort Wayne, Indiana, then taken a job on Seventh Avenue as "just another designer in the back room." But soon he crawled out from under the wing of Jane Derby, a southern belle who made pretty clothes but was more at home in Bermuda than in the workaday world of fashion, and established himself as one of the first big names in American fashion—following the great Norell on the East Coast and James Galanos on the West Coast. Bill Blass moved slowly off Seventh Avenue and quickly into the social world of his clients. He was the first Seventh Avenue designer (aside from Mainbocher, who was still stuck in the custom business, dressing C. Z. Guest, Babe Paley, and friends) to sit at the tables of New York's élite—the Paleys, the Whitneys, and the Queen of New York, Elsie Woodward. Norell had never moved in these circles, and Galanos, considered by some to be one of the most important American designers, lived quietly in the canyons of Los Angeles, hatching his strategy of waiting until Milan, Paris, and the New York shows were over and then trundling into New York with his clothes—the best made in the U.S., and the most expensive.

Blass and Mainbocher were the first to forge a natural relationship between designer and customer. Blass charmed his camp of women into wearing his clothes. When former first lady Nancy Reagan went to Russia, she consulted Blass on her wardrobe. "What do I wear to the Gorbachevs' dacha outside Moscow when we dine informally?" Blass, of course, had the answer: "Something simple."

Last year Barbara Bush, surrounded by secret service agents, stopped off at the Blass showroom before she hit the campaign trail.

When Bill leaves his stone house in Connecticut (an old tavern, where, Bill says, George Washington once stopped) and takes to the open road, he travels as a true celebrity. Across the land, women with money line up to buy his clothes and to greet their fashion hero. On his sixty-sixth birthday, Blass was in Texas, and his "gals" there—who just love "Willie"—gave him a Lone Star birthday party to remember.

Blass's only real rival on the social scene is his good friend Oscar de la Renta, but Oscar is more the Latin lover type, while Blass might best be described as a pseudo English gentleman. Blass, when uneasy, unconsciously generates a slight English accent. When smoking he also stiffens up, somewhat in the manner of Ronald Colman, who was no slouchy dresser himself.

Blass's fashion? American in concept; sophisticated in the sense that he makes a sporty look respectable for older women. His final silhouette—the key to fashion—like that of all other designers, is generally inspired by Paris; but Blass can out-Paris Paris sometimes by taking a sophisticated French idea and making it more wearable and just as attractive for the American woman. His clothes, incidentally, look best on tall women—e.g., Nancy Kissinger—and especially for evening, he can design "knock 'em dead" dresses that wear exceedingly well in Texas or California, where women want to be seen but not necessarily heard from.

After coming back from a road show, Blass jumps into his Lincoln station wagon (he is given a new one every year for designing what the manufacturer calls the "Blass Lincoln"), lights up a cigarette, and, together with his chauffeur, barrels off to his Connecticut tavern, where he is happiest to be alone with his two favorites, Shelby and Kate, golden retrievers, who sleep on his bed. With his two best friends at his side, Bill Blass no longer has to charm anyone.

Once designers have established an image in the eyes of their customers, the stores, and, of course, the press, they are stuck with their own idea of themselves. Having an image means that in interviews they usually have to repeat the same designer truisms over and over again:

"My ideal woman is So-and-so" (depending on the season).

"I believe in elegance."

"Clothes that are practical."

"I'm against pants,"

"I'm for pants."

"I went to . . . and that's where I became inspired."

"Enough of long."

"Short."

"Short and long."

"Just give me a natural look."

"A tougher look."

"Hair should be short and natural."

"Black stockings."

"Light beige."

"No hats."

"Big hats."

"Wide shoulders and pads."

"Natural shoulders."

And so on ad infinitum.

But as we've noted before, underneath all this fashion talk is a deep well of basic insecurity. Until the last moment, designers aren't sure what they are going to make or even how they want women to look. Four times a year they have to face facts: there has to be a change, not enough to capsize the boat but just enough so that women are tempted to buy a new body cover. With all this insecurity and in their anxiety over portraying the "right" image, designers as a form of relief often overindulge in some of the best things in life: houses, paintings, furniture, boats, vacations, food, and sex. In fact, I cannot think of one well-known designer who lives what you and I might call a simple or even a normal life.

Item: Gianni Versace, whose clothes sell like hotcakes in his native Italy but not outside that country, leaves his Mongiardino-decorated palazzo in Milan, or his Lake Como villa, and takes a caravan of companions to live in the Libyan desert. At night, in their luxurious tents, they feast on tinned delicacies, and under a sky spangled with stars they dance to rock 'n' roll in the dunes.

Item: Giorgio Armani's country estate at Broni, an hour from Milan, is so huge that the staff travel by bicycle, and Armani himself uses a golf cart to go from pool house to main house to the part of the stables he has converted into a small dining room, its walls covered with pictures of him as a young child. At night, for security, an iron gate grinds down from the top of the roof to seal off the house completely.

Item: In a span of two weeks, Oscar de la Renta flies behind the iron curtain on Sid Bass's private jet—Prague, East Berlin, Potsdam, Dresden, and then on to Turkey. Days before, he has been in Paris, the South of France, Marseilles, and Madrid. Then it is back to New York, before leaving for Salzburg for the music festival in August.

Item: Carolyne Roehm, who was Oscar's assistant designer until he introduced her to Henry Kravis, now her husband, one of America's wealthiest tycoons, is off to Moscow—you guessed it—on another private jet. Next year off again private jetting to India.

Item: Hubert de Givenchy, who in his way may be the grandest of all the designers, leaves his beautiful Paris apartment at the Hôtel Bauffremont, on the rue de Grenelle, for a sail on his yacht through Greece and Turkey.

Item: Karl Lagerfeld, a German eighteenth-century man who describes himself as *nouveau pauvre,* is decorating his villa in Monte Carlo—a lifetime gift from Prince Rainier—to museum standards. The cost: $40 million. Lagerfeld, who has just completed an apartment in Rome and is still working on his château in Brittany, has earned his luxury: each year he turns out for Chanel two couture collections and two ready-to-wear collections, as well as two fur and ready-to-wear sportswear collections for the Fendi sisters of Rome, and two collections for his own German company— plus an in-between line of clothes.

Item: Emanuel Ungaro has spent over two years restoring a house deep in the wilds of Provence, complete with a twelfth-century chapel. There, he intends to stage classical concerts that will resound throughout the valley.

Item: Christian Lacroix, his career just beginning, lives simply in a rented Paris apartment, unable to decide whether to buy there or instead to buy a house near his native Arles.

Item: Claude Montana, who even in the heat of Capri summers turns himself into a cowboy with his shiny leather pants, blue denim jacket, and pointy American cowboy boots, is restoring a small villa in Capri—as well as a house outside of Paris.

Item: Thierry Mugler takes fine photographs, including photographs of his own clothes, in different parts of the world.

Item: Pierre Cardin circles the globe, checking on his em- pire—Maxim's Restaurants, Maxim's Hotel, Cardin fashion licensees—and for a few weekends of rest goes to his vil- lage in the South of France, where he talks to his animals, especially his exotic birds and his six collies.

These designers live better lives than most of their clients, usually more original and more stylish. Their homes are exquisitely decorated (although often overdone, be- cause of their inherent fashiony nature). They usually hire decorators: Valentino, the American Peter Marino; Gianni Versace, the Italian Mongiardino; Yves Saint Laurent, fel- low Frenchman Jacques Grange; Oscar de la Renta uses three: the Frenchman Vincent Fourcade, Thierry Despont, and the American doyenne Sister Parrish. Then, working with their decorators, they add their own touches, so that when the houses are finished, they are decorated to perfec- tion.

Some designers—Givenchy, Ungaro, and Lagerfeld—do the decorating themselves. Bill Blass, who mostly stays at home in America ("I hate to travel to Europe, but he writes for *Traveler* magazine), does his own houses and no longer uses Mica Ertegun and Chessy Rayner, two American decorators who have made a big business out of fixing up the interiors of banks and offices.

Blass is a great shopper, and he is always searching for one-of-a-kind Swedish furniture and English paintings and drawings. He scours the New York antique shops, and what he doesn't use he sends to storage.

Oscar de la Renta cannot resist an auction. One year he buys Orientalist paintings, only to put them on the block for a profit a few months later, changing his apartment style as fast as he can design a new collection.

For a designer, living well is part of an overall drive always to display good taste. Blass, who collects paintings and drawings aided by the sharp eye of art expert and author John Richardson, has a warehouse full of acquisitions, as does Saint Laurent, who doesn't remember what he owns.

And because designers often have a keen interest in art, decorating, and living in a civilized manner, they are watched carefully by the social world. True to their tradition, some designers, such as Saint Laurent, Ungaro, Blass, de la Renta, and Lagerfeld, attract attention not only for their clothes but because of the way they live. The life-style publications fight over their homes, and even their offices, because they are always changing their surroundings as they move gracefully from house to house, sensitive to the beauty of every room and every plant in their gardens. It means nothing to de la Renta to replant overnight an entire garden at his home in Santo Domingo, or to bring in fullsize pines to the wild fields of his seventy-acre Connecticut estate. For the placement of these pines and the general layout of the garden, he hired the late Russell Page, a landscape architect whose consulting fee used to be $1,000 an hour. Not far away, Carolyne Roehm Kravis is redoing her own garden with old trees approximating the specimens in Central Park.

Nouvelle Society, Old Money, and even some of the rest of us not only are dressed by these sacred designers but are inspired in other ways as well—in home decorating, the collecting of antiques and art, menus, traveling, and even deciding what is In and what is Out. The designers have become our experts in civilized living. And to think that not so long ago they were only dressing women and were not even invited to supper!

From tradesmen to masters of style, the important designers are sought after more than most other celebrities because we've come to believe that they can show us how to enjoy the finer things of life. Understand, I'm not saying that designers are the most educated, the most fascinating, or the best-informed people in the world, but there is little doubt that their contribution to our living well is considerable. Simply because they are always looking for that "something new"—which probably does not exist—the top designers are stimulating and fun to know. Except when they get on the subject of fashion, about which they can be truly boring.

Fashion is a sub-art and is not intellectual. Fashion is a business and operates best when it is born out of instinct. Fashion appeals to the senses and comes from gut feeling. Forget the fashion intellectuals who blow hard about the logic and history of fashion. True fashion comes straight out of the jungle.

To satisfy their hunger for more and more objects, houses, gardens, art, and entertainment, designers have turned to licensing their names, which certainly goes a long way to support their extravagant life-styles. But as they spend more and more, and gather newer riches along the way, there is always the danger that their high life can end abruptly should their licensing agreements fail to produce huge incomes for their manufacturers. Balenciaga, one of the greats, ended his days with little money. Christian Dior and Coco Chanel, after their enormous commercial successes, didn't leave fortunes, by any means. Dior and Chanel, however, did leave a great legacy to the owners of their respective businesses. Alain Wertheimer, the owner of Chanel, and now Financière Agache, the owner of Dior, have both made fortunes out of the Chanel and Dior names.

And—talk about nightmares—staring the designer in the face every day is the fear that suddenly his name will lose all its allure for the general public. So publicity and advertising to keep that name out front are essential to continuing success. And as the designer needs more and more money, so does the licenser demand more and more. The big-name designers talk about their licensees like this: "I get a million dollars for sheets a year" (Bill Blass). "Avon raised my royalty on perfumes half a percentage point and is asking for more personal appearances" (Oscar de la Renta). For de la Renta, his take from perfume royalties edges into the $3 million bracket. De la Renta's name appears on shoes, eyeglasses, men's clothing, cashmere from Scotland, belts, jewelry, cosmetics, men's fragrances, and, last but not least, soon on Oscar de la Renta oranges and juice from his plantation in the Dominican Republic.

From Saint Laurent there are cigarettes, and in the future, wines, liquor, and automobiles. (Givenchy and Blass already have their names on Lincolns.) Designer names can end up on almost anything, even, as with Cardin, on bathroom fixtures. Pierre Cardin, the inventor of designer licensing, sees his name plastered around the world; even clothes for the Chinese and the Russians bear his label. When Cardin bought Maxim's, his fashion rivals scoffed, but he cleaned up the front room, built a new kitchen, and packed one of Paris's once great restaurants to the rafters with tourists and the new French rich. Maxim's in Paris isn't what it used to be—I have seen a soccer player remove his jacket in the middle of dinner—but then is anything the same? (There are also Maxim's now in Moscow, Tokyo, New York, and Beijing. During the student uprising in June 1989 the People's Army briefly occupied Cardin's Maxim's in Beijing.)

To run their licensing empires, the top designers hire executives whose job it is to keep their manufacturers happy with the contract, though one cannot always say the designers are paying close attention to what the name goes on. Cardin boasts of a design studio in Paris that is supposed to pass on everything bearing the Cardin logo, but as the designers and their manufacturers become greedier and greedier, the quality can slip to mediocre and below. As long as the designer name sells, no one seems to care. Then, too, a man like Saint Laurent has no real interest in following the fortunes of his name all over the world. Not if the fortune keeps coming to him. With Cardin, it's different. With 254 licensing agreements, Cardin is rarely out of a plane; he flies around the world more than twice a year.

On that dark day when a designer's name fades from glory, his manufacturers can jump ship quickly, and the rich designer can become poor almost overnight. No wonder the press has such a powerful position in the life of any designer: he can live or die by the number of pages he can command. All the top designers have enormous publicity machines, which are in constant touch with fashion editors and others; however, the only couturiers and designers to make the covers of *Time* and *Newsweek* have been the late Christian Dior, Giorgio Armani, Yves Saint Laurent, Christian Lacroix, and Ralph Lauren. Carolyne Roehm was on the August 1989 cover of *Fortune,* not as a designer but as the second wife of CEO Henry Kravis.

But even more than the perils and pitfalls of licensing, what concerns me is that there are no new big-name designers coming along—not because of lack of talent but because to get started anywhere today in the fashion business

requires enormous capital. The thought that fashion hangs
by the thread spun by Saint Laurent, Ungaro, Lagerfeld, and
a few others gives one pause and worry. What will happen
after the greats are gone? What if the best of them just get
tired and decide to rest on their laurels? To support his life
style, Hubert de Givenchy sold his empire, on September 8,
1988, for 225 million French francs. Emanuel Ungaro, who
began with nothing and who is still bravely struggling,
would like to have a rich and powerful partner to help him
along. His business was partly held by Sonya Knapp, a Swiss
who once worked with and was romantically linked to him.
She has reluctantly given up Emanuel and her shares in his
business.

Of even greater concern to me is the possibility that, with
the Paris couture barely surviving, designer names could
become an anachronism in our time. Marc Bohan, who,
with Saint Laurent, has the greatest number of private customers, lamented the other day: "We just cannot get the
delivery of original and exclusive fabrics anymore, because
the mills only want to work for ready-to-wear. After all, we
cannot sell all of our six-thousand-dollar suits in gray
flannel!!"

Without the special fabrics and without the trained hands
to cut and sew and with fewer and fewer customers (even
those women with the time and money find couture fittings
"a bore"), the couture as we know it faces an uncertain
future. If the couture dies out, where will future designers
seed and grow? And most important of all, what will happen to the wonderful couture laboratory, where a designer
can experiment on a coat, suit, or dress that will be copied
around the world?

In 1988, Lacroix showed a loss of $8 million, even though
his sales had grown fourfold over the previous year. Those
figures alone show how difficult it is to make money out of
high fashion. Yet there are those who are still convinced
that they will. Bernard Arnault, chairman of LVMH, which

controls Lacroix (as well as Dior, Givenchy, and Vuitton) says: "Lacroix has the potential to become the premier name in haute couture in the next decade. If that happens, and with the launch of a perfume, ours will be seen as a first-rate investment."

The fashion "experts" have been saying that the Paris, Milan, and New York designers will come forth in their ready-to-wear with the new ideas that will keep fashion alive. Yet the prices for top ready-to-wear fashion are also shooting out of sight.

Frankly, I don't believe that sterile fashion will take over. Real women don't want blue Mao jackets and baggy work pants. They want to be different—savagely competitive—to keep ahead and to capture their man. And the creative fashion designers, even though they are almost an endangered species, will survive because women will still want to look great—or at least better than other women.

The antifashion trend is a tough problem for creative designers. As I write these lines, Emanuel Ungaro struggles to complete his couture collection in four weeks' time. He telephones: "I'm suffering, John, really suffering to find my way. Anyway, my look is going to be simple. So simple."

As long as there are Ungaros who are suffering to give fashion new life, the creative spirit will never die; and so long as there are women who appreciate beauty in fashion and who want to be beautiful themselves, high couture will continue to ornament our changing world.

FASHION BEGINS
WITH THE SKETCHES

YVESSAINTLAURENT

W AT SAINT LAURENT WINTER 1990

A Tage of Brocard
SPLASH OF COLORS

ungaro

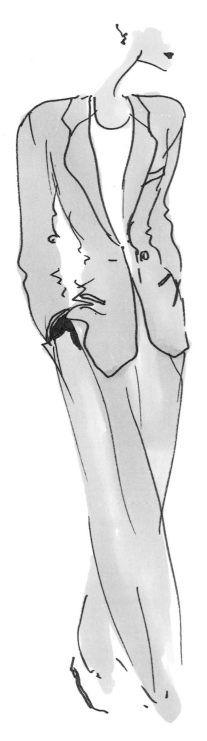

GIORGIO ARMANI

nowaday fashion. CLLno

NO MORE DIKTATS! FASHION IS FREEDOM!
When Mrs Minimal-conservative meets
Miss Ethnic-Mix&Match and Miss Casual

Karl Lagerfeld

DONNAKARAN

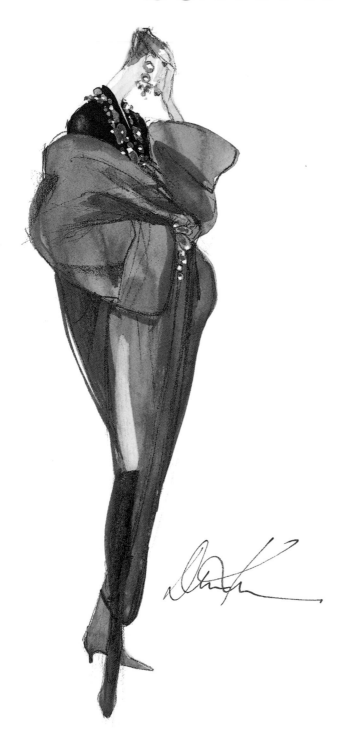

MARC BOHAN

RALPH LAUREN

Scaasi

Givenchy

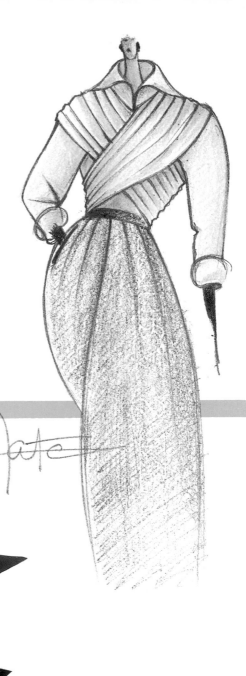

GianniVersace

1

2

Everyone can be a fashion victim including many of the famous ladies on these pages: Nancy Kissinger (1), Princess Di (2), Pat Buckley (3), Annette Reed (4), LouLou Klossowski (5), Marie-Hélène de Rothschild (6), and Mica Ertegun (7).

Marie-Hélène de Rothschild is merchandising her own perfume with Revlon—you guessed it: "Marie-Hélène."

3

4

5

6

7

2

4

3

Everyone loves a bride, and ending every Paris show are the wedding dresses that are sometimes out of this world. In the big photo, a Bohan wedding dress (1); on the left, another Bohan wedding dress (2); the dress with a crown, Emanuel Ungaro (3); and above, Christian Lacroix (4).

5   6

A YSL of course (5), a Montana fantasy wedding next to it (6), and below, Inès, for Chanel by Lagerfeld (7).

7

KRIZIA

4
PLAYING SAVAGE GAMES

A s much as the rest of the world complains about the Island of Manhattan and its evil ways, for me Manhattan has an allure, a magnetic hold when I'm there, struggling like all the rest of those savage Manhattan Islanders. But when I'm away, the attraction dies—and quickly. I don't miss the dirty streets, the smelly garbage bags piled high, and the rats that run outside our apartment building. It is part of Manhattan philosophy to put up with all the hardships—to complain night and day and still come back for more. Why?

As I ride uptown to luncheon at La Grenouille (today, the traffic turns it into a forty-five-minute trip from our office at 7 East Twelfth Street), the cabdriver says to me, "New York is a wonderful town." The springs in the seat are sticking me, the cab smells of urine and cigarette butts, yet the driver is full of enthusiasm. Unlike some of those in Paris who snarl their way through the gridlocks of that beautiful city. When I reach La Grenouille, see the sun streaming through the big front window, and receive a warm greeting from Charles Masson, the young owner, and Joseph, his headwaiter, I decide that perhaps today the cabdriver is right. Looking around the still-empty room—I always arrive promptly at twelve-thirty both to escape the rush and because the food is better—I see the masses of flowers stretching to the ceiling. There is dirt and brutality outside in this great city, but New Yorkers have learned to create beautiful environments inside, secure, warm nests, even friendly ones. So a big cheer for New York, a city where, if you can afford it, you dine better and in a finer environment than in most cities in the world. Simply put, New York has it all, good and bad, so let's talk about them both.

Behind the façade of the rich and powerful, there lurks a fear that New York could easily erupt, spilling the kind of violent hatred and class warfare into the streets that Tom Wolfe portrayed in his novel *The Bonfire of the Vanities*. Homeless sleep on the steps of St. James Church or prop themselves up against fashionable Park Avenue apartment houses. The haves and have-nots are always with you in New York. Outside La Côte Basque, or any of those smart New York restaurants, the street is piled high with black, dreary garbage bags. If you leave the restaurant late enough, you will see a burly sanitation man sliding those bags along the sidewalk, a reminder that underneath New York's glittering façade lies another world, not nearly as pretty.

Many of us are shielded from these unpleasant everyday

happenings. The back elevator man clears away our garbage and filth; the white-gloved front doorman opens the door for us and hails the taxi or the private limousine. New York is full of fine outward trappings. Nevertheless, when I walked near Carl Schurz Park and saw rats crossing my path and read signs warning that rat poison had been put down, I couldn't wait to get back to the security of our apartment overlooking the East River. And when my wife, Jill, told me that the nannies in the park tell the children to "look at the squirrels" but they're pointing at rats, I joined those who wonder what New York is coming to. But I don't join Tom Wolfe in his depiction of everyone in New York as completely evil. New Yorkers *are* tough, but in their struggle to survive they are as good as anyone else—or better. They're alive and ready to try any new idea at all costs —sometimes too quick to abandon the old. Probably the most important job of a New Yorker is first to survive—and then to have staying power.

All the changes, what is In and what is Out, make our job at the newspaper exciting most of the time, and fatiguing some of it. The stars of our pages are born and fade away very quickly.

How do all the Ins and Outs really take place? We at *W* are supposed to be able to answer that question. Sometimes, people give us credit or blame for "creating" the characters who live in our pages throughout the year. But these people create themselves. They *want* to be seen and heard, to appear everywhere, to be photographed even in their own homes, or at dinners and luncheons in the restaurants they consider "fashionable": Le Cirque for the Nouvelles (as we came to call them), La Côte Basque for the Wobbly Wasps (of whom more later), La Grenouille for non-showoffs (except on Saturday nights, when the patrons cross the river from New Jersey, ready to flash their diamonds and chew their cigars), Bellini's on the West Side and Bice on the East Side for the fashion establishment, and Lutèce for the rich who prefer to remain Invisible. But even these Invisible are photographed by *W* at the charity balls, reported on by *The New York Times* (sometimes grudgingly because the women in Larchmont might not understand), and written about by columnist Suzy, who glowingly approves of all social events whether she's amused or bored silly.

What the social world of New York really comes down to is that anyone—and I mean anyone—can become an overnight attraction of *W* or of the gossip columns if he or she has enough money and stamina. And don't listen to any of the leaders of society who say, "We can't stand publicity." Most of them thrive on seeing their names in the papers. Sneak into the bedrooms of the high and mighty early on a New York morning and you can catch them turning first to Liz Smith's gossip column in the New York *Daily News.* Before they have their tea, they're checking out Suzy in the New York *Post* to see whether they're mentioned. Their excuse is always the same ("Well, you know Alfred and I really don't like publicity, but we have to let the press help our favorite charity"). Every morning at the office, we're swamped with invitations to this or that charity event— sometimes ten a night during the height of the season—and like lemmings our reporters are off and running to cover these events, even though we know all of them will be attended by the same people. To a fashion designer or anyone connected with the fashion world, these affairs mean more clothes, and thus more money in the bank.

There are actually some social New Yorkers who never stay home unless they're too sick to go out. I have seen Pat Buckley, a princess of New York, spreading her joy and laughter, though on crutches for more than a year. But Jill and I just don't go. After a day at the office hearing about last night's social events, it is a pleasure to be home by ourselves or out for a quiet dinner with friends. The biggest luxury in New York is peace and quiet. The only place to find it is in your own home, and even that's difficult, what with the city symphony of ambulances, fire trucks, and police cars. But that is still better than the noise in the restaurants these days, where there's no way to have a sensible conversation above the din.

Still, I have to admit that the talk at these restaurants can be fun sometimes. Take a dinner Jill and I had at The Four Seasons in the Bar Room (which, at the time, was suddenly In for dinner). The Bar Room is like a paneled basketball court with a striped rug, but at least you can hear yourself talk there. The conversation will be something special tonight, I tell myself, as the headwaiter rams a bulky metal chair into the back of my legs. For a high-toned group has been assembled: twelve of us—Pat and Bill Buckley; Oscar de la Renta; Annette Reed; Mary and Swifty Lazar (thank God Swifty's paying the bill, with wine going for $5.75 a glass); Mica and Ahmet Ertegun, fresh from their rock-'n'-roll Hall of Fame evening; and most important, Sid Bass and Mercedes Kellogg. Mercedes is constantly in motion, full of touches as she grabs people here and there.

The play begins. First the gossip. They are talking about John and Susan Gutfreund, the first of Nouvelle Society to break upon the New York scene, but now poised under the guillotine of the press. The august *New York Times* and razor-sharp *New York* Magazine have both run long pieces on the Gutfreunds' frivolous ways and on John Gutfreund's ruthless behavior at Salomon Brothers, once one of New York's most powerful investment-banking houses. So right now there's big trouble for the Gutfreunds, but those in the Bar Room this evening know that the guillotine could fall on any one of them. It's a chilling thought.

I think about seeing the Gutfreunds at La Grenouille on a Saturday, having lunch alone, very much tête-à-tête, Susan maintaining a stiff upper lip. And then a week later there she was on the Concorde, winging her way to Paris with her secretary and little John, Jr., who sat in the back of the

Concorde cabin with his nanny while Mummy rode sepa-
rately.

"If he sees me on the plane all he wants to do is play,"
she told her travel agent, who delivered her to the airport
and took care of the passports, the boarding cards, and the
mounds of luggage for the Gutfreund entourage as they
headed for their Paris residence on the rue de Grenelle,
attempting to outwait—and outwit—the press guillotine
another day.

Back to our dinner. After we finish with the Gutfreunds,
some real food, and a new Italian wine, no one wants to
talk about world problems and everyone is bored with politics. Clothes they don't discuss, they just buy them.
Mercedes Kellogg, who has one eye on Sid Bass while he's
talking to Jill, and the other on Oscar de la Renta, doesn't
know it yet, but she and Annette Reed are both wearing the
same dress and the same black coat from the very same
Oscar, the favorite designer of Nouvelle Society. The wine
goes upstairs, straight to everyone's head. It's time for fun,
children's fun.

Ahmet Ertegun, who has invented a few things in his day
in addition to Atlantic Records, says, "Let's start a hotel."

"I'll be the switchboard operator," says Mary Lazar.

"I want to be the cook," says Pat Buckley.

"No, I'm the cook," says Oscar de la Renta, who always
gets his way. They both agree to be in the kitchen.

Mercedes Kellogg, who is on her fifth cigarillo, says in her
throaty Persian accent, "I'm the barman."

Bill Buckley, who finds the whole hotel discussion tedi-
ous, is told, "Bill, you'll be in charge of reservations."

"That's no good," someone says. He'll be so busy writing
on his computer he'll forget and we won't have any guests."

Trouble-maker that I am, no one has offered me a job. I
state that I'll work in the hotel only if Sid Bass puts up the
money, owns it, and runs it. Finally Ahmet Ertegun decides
that I will give rumba lessons. Annette Reed, who is also

unemployed, is told by her friend Oscar de la Renta, "You can make the beds." Talk about noise! The few other people in the restaurant cannot believe all the screaming and howling. In one of the Four Seasons' booths, an older gentleman is on the telephone, surrounded by four women of the night. He can hardly hear his conversation. The headwaiter tells me, "Your group is really something special." Are we?

As we get up to leave we decide to call our venture Hotel Paradiso. All together, we skip down the Four Seasons' grand staircase and out into the New York night, far now from any touch of paradise, and as we pile into the limousines purring at the curb, we seem to sense that New York is changing—for the worse.

But now there is really no change. New York is becoming even more intense. The new Nouvelles have taken over from the old Nouvelles—the Nouvelles of yesterday giving up to those who have more money and energy.

It is all like the children's game of Snakes and Ladders, in which the object is to climb to the top of the ladder while avoiding the snakes along the way that can set you back to the beginning. Let's see how it is played by the Savage Set in an age in which money and power get you into the game, but you are always in danger of being replaced by someone who has more.

Lay out the Snakes and Ladders game board and get ready to roll the dice. They fall to the board: a four and a three—lucky seven.

Move seven spaces to lunch at Le Cirque, then go back two spaces. Double six—great! A telegraphed invitation to the Sid Bass–Mercedes Kellogg pre-wedding dinner at the Metropolitan Museum; advance one space. (An aside: After the ceremony, Texas tycoon Bass kissed the bride and yelled "Yahoo.") *W* ran the saga of the Bass wedding under the headline HOW MERCEDES HOOKED HER BASS. Funny—not really—go back three spaces. Roll. Two. Fly to Annenberg 350-acre Palm Springs estate (with private golf course) for the last—as President—New Year's Eve dinner with Nancy and Ronald Reagan. The twentieth time the Reagans have welcomed in the New Year with the King and Queen of California Nouvelle. Back one. Travel to the party on Malcolm Forbes's private jet with Brooke Astor, Walker Jerry Zipkin, investor Alecko Papamarkou (the man who can arrange anything). Swallowed by a snake. Go back to beginning and try again. Roll hard this time. Invited to shoot quail at the Farish ranch in Texas with the President-elect. Advance ten spaces to the bottom of the ladder. The Farishes are Invisible People who are now in the news because of their friendship with the Bushes. Even Queen Elizabeth II has laid her weary royal head on the Farish pillows at their horse-breeding farm, and the Queen rarely sleeps in the home of a commoner.

Roll a four. Betsy Bloomingdale wears the dress Jerry Zipkin advised to the Bedford Ball. She's out on the dance floor, singing "Just a gigolo."

An important throw: four and one. *Eau de carotte*—that's the secret perfume concocted for Washington socialite Evangeline Bruce, and with a throw of five we are about to discover the Paris perfumer who created this special scent. Ahead five but still not near the ladder.

Be fortunate enough to have been at La Côte Basque with the late Hebe Dorsey, who asked questions better than any other reporter, to have been on hand to hear her ask Ivana Trump what she thought of her husband's purported entrance into the political arena, and to hear Ivana, clad in a bright emerald sequined dress, respond, "I don't like my private life being exposed, so deep down I'm against it. But then, how many houses and buildings can you erect and decorate?" Move ahead two. Just missed another snake.

Roll a two and one and lunch at The Four Seasons Bar

Room, where Julian, the wittiest headwaiter in New York, offers pasta with white truffles picked by his friend in Lucca and served with virgin olive oil from Tuscany. Move closer to the ladder, but still four to go to reach it.

Snake eyes. In Southampton tear down a large cottage: the Ahmet Erteguns did but could not find anyone to take the debris away. Decorator Mica wants to build a Russian dacha like Yves Saint Laurent's in Deauville. Go back four spaces. Will we ever get up that ladder? Six and one. Lunch at Mortimer's. Meat loaf and Connecticut sweet, smooth relish made especially for Mortimer's owner Glenn Bernbaum, who still offers the best value in town at his restaurant, which is run like a private club: an "Unknown" is kept waiting for a table even when the restaurant is half empty. We've made the first rung on the ladder because Pat Buckley, the Florence Nightingale of New York charities as well as the Bea Lillie of the New York scene, is lunching at Mortimer's at the same time (even though we have been placed in the second room, where we can hear the empty bottles dropping into the waste can).

Roll. One and one. Attending the Metropolitan Museum Costume Institute Ball, wear an Oscar de la Renta. Ahead one. A Bill Blass polka-dot number, go back two spaces. Go ahead six in your Arnold Scaasi, the always favorite designer of the Wasps and now the choice of First Lady Barbara. But next year even in your Scaasi you can expect to go back ten spaces if you attend the Costume Institute Ball at the Metropolitan. One of the world's greatest museums has fallen prey to its own greed in trying to raise more and more money at all costs.

Marietta Tree's cocktail party for English painter Teddy Millington Drake: go up the ladder one. Book party for Richard Clurman at Mortimer's, back two. Opening night at the Metropolitan Opera: back six. Try again.

Literary Lions Dinner at the New York Public Library, go ahead six. You are again approaching the ladder and going up. Ahead four if you are at Brooke Astor's table with her; back two if you are at her second table.

With a roll of six and four you land lunch at The Four Seasons (Bar Room, of course). James Wolfensohn, Australian-born investment banker, nods "Hello." Go ahead four. Lazard Frères banker Felix Rohatyn and his wife, Liz (he is about the only Wall Street tycoon who appears at The Four Seasons with his wife), are lunching with Brooke Astor, who is wearing one of her Zasu Pitts crazy hats. The three of them wave. Go ahead five. Tom Wolfe in his vanilla ice-cream suit is sitting upstairs in the Four Seasons balcony, observing the jungle feeding scene below him. Leonard Lauder, cosmetics king, huddles in the center booth with media tycoon Si Newhouse, who barely acknowledges Rupert Murdoch, his arch rival, who huddles with four henchmen. Roll the dice and stop the gossip and play the game. Order California chardonnay Talbot (a Carmel Valley wine being pushed by the wine merchants). Another snake. Go back seven spaces.

With the new roll you fly to London, stay at the Connaught: ahead four; lunch at Claridge's, back six; dinner at Harry's Bar, ahead five; return on the British Concorde in time for breakfast at the Hotel Carlyle, ahead three. Six and one, a lucky seven and off for a February weekend at Hobe Sound in Florida, where you see Douglas and Kay Kay Auchincloss, who forget where they last parked their Mercedes station wagon. You don't see Drue Heinz, widow of Jack Heinz (57 Varieties), because she is selling her houses (Hobe Sound and Ascot are already gone for $12 million). In front of her Sutton Place townhouse police barricades have closed off the square "so the chauffeurs don't sleep and park." Determined Drue, once one of the more visible of New York's social leaders, still wields her power, as she did in years gone by when she served the Queen of England a ketchup sorbet.

And so the game goes on, the Savage Set striving to get to

the top of the ladder—reaching for power, social position, respectability, all by being with the right people in the right places at the right times. They keep rolling the dice, moving up and down, sometimes ending up winners of the game but not necessarily winners in life.

5
SAVAGE
PUBLISHING

As in fashion, there has been a dramatic change in our type of publishing since Fairchild Publications was founded more than seventy-five years ago. We too are struggling to survive in a competitive marketplace, where the consumer, or in our case the reader, rightfully has become much more demanding.

Thanks to the revolution in the ways of communication, there is so much more information available and readers are so bombarded from all sides that there is almost too much to read. To add to our problems, Americans are not big readers. They favor the visual, with a minimum amount of reading. They want information quickly, want the best and the newest right away, before someone else gets it first. They are sick of bad news, world news, sick to death of politicians and politics. It is the trappings of power and the human suffering of celebrities and of the "élite" that fascinates them. No wonder even the august *New York Times* and its rival in journalistic quality, the *Washington Post,* devote pages to style and personality profiles. Even the *Wall Street Journal* in its two front-page column stories has run such surprising subjects as "what to do about gout" or a profile of Yves Saint Laurent.

We decided to specialize in the areas we knew best. Our first priority has always been to cover events as they occur but to put the emphasis on the people who keep life pulsating. How people live, how they conduct their business, how they have become successful, how they have solved problems, how they relate to others—all of this is very important but even more important is to describe their human element: how they enjoy life, all phases of their work and play. Readers want to feel they are witnesses to the drama.

Covering style in every aspect—people style, living style, working style, playing style, romantic style, business style, even that boring subject political style—style both good and bad is part of the new journalism.

The readers want to visualize in full color a world they don't necessarily know, want to dream and to fantasize: "Wouldn't I like to live like that"; "Wouldn't I like to look like that"; "Oh, I want that dress." Or they may decide: "What a ridiculous fast phony world that is. Thank God I'm right here in Greenwich, Connecticut, with my dog and cat." But at least I hope they read on.

We want to make our readers smile, laugh at themselves, at others and at us. And we try always to be first with the romance of life: to let our readers see the new Saint Laurent dress before it is even shown in Paris, before the last pins have been removed from the hem, to share an interview with Nancy Reagan when she entered the White House and another just before she left, to see Jackie Onassis lunching at The Four Seasons, to read of Michel David-Weill of Lazard Frères, one of the world's brightest bankers, at home on the Riviera, to see Christian Lacroix creating his new collection, to hear of Gianni and Marella Agnelli, to learn the real story of Pamela Harriman.

We invent fashion terms like "hot pants" and social terms like "Nouvelle Society." We discover new restaurants, write about the flowers at La Grenouille, list the newest wines, describe how the young vintners live in Bordeaux, how a forester works in the Swiss Alps, depict a day in the life of English poet Sir Stephen Spender, tell of the Young Royals of Britain, and—of course—cover what's In and what's Out, the list we invented.

The world of *W* has to do with style. "Style is idiosyncrasy. Anything that goes against the trend." That definition comes from my son-in-law, Peter Melhado. My family and I were eating breakfast outside in the South of France. We were having fresh eggs from our chickens, drinking coffee from blue-and-yellow Giverny cups, sitting at a table covered with a yellow-and-white Indian seersucker tablecloth, while enjoying baguettes, cherries, apricots, and fresh cherry jam—and being shielded from the June sun by overhanging Concord grapes.

I had just gotten stuck on these lines about style, so I had put my family to work for me: Jill, my wife, all in white with a large straw hat, Jillie, our daughter, in Bermuda shorts, Jillie's twin brother, Stephen, a designer, in a washed-corduroy baggy sweat shirt and purple glasses.

"What is style anyway?" I asked. Peter explained, "At M.K. [at the moment the In nightclub–dinner spot for the élite young] everyone is wearing the same uniform, tight black clothes with boots. The men and women all look alike. That is a style." Stephen agreed: The women want to be men and the men want to look more like women. Perhaps the Michael Jackson or David Bowie influence."

"Who has style?" I asked. "Hard to find women with real style," Stephen said. "Maybe Grace Kelly." Someone groaned. Jillie: "Stephen Spender with his white hair and big straw hat askew, he has style." We agreed. Then I said, "The English I think have the most style." Jill: "They do. Nothing to do with the way they dress, but the way they act, the way they think gives them style." Jill told us that her candidate for a man with real style was Gianni Agnelli: "Perfect manners, charming, and the way he looked just perfect wearing blue jeans and a blue jean jacket when he arrived, and then in the evening changed to the perfect double-breasted blazer with gold buttons, the whitest shirt, red-and-blue ascot scarf, and emerald-green corduroy pants, freshly polished loafers." What a rave. I was jealous, really jealous, and was about to counter that Marella Agnelli, his wife, is a woman with great style. But they were through with the subject and off to the pool, our pool built with old Provençal stone but ruined because when the cement walls started crumbling, our French architect, who is mad for American technology, sprayed the sides with a white plastic substance—ugh. So it's all a matter of style good or bad, isn't it?

In the beginning, our idea was to report on all styles. But generally we write about those who have fine style, who are stylish, though sometimes we write about those who just think they have style.

My father always reminded me that style and fashion were to be found in everything from clothes to food to the way we all live. To him, everything and everyone had style, although he disapproved of anything frivolous and ostentatious.

His legacy to me, simply put, was to print "news and ideas." We have not changed that much, even though Capital Cities/ABC, Inc. has bought the company. Now we are thirty-one publications strong, still printing, we hope, unique news and ideas.

In my early conversations with Tom Murphy, chief executive officer of Capital Cities/ABC, Inc., he asked what we had in mind for the future. I mentioned our ideas for a new publication—*W*—meant to take from *WWD* the best of the material about high fashion—and high-fashion living—for the consumer. We had waked up one day to find that socialites and people like Jacqueline Onassis, who had always denied she read *WWD* when she was in the White House, were reading us. We had a hard-core consumer circulation. We had had to change *WWD* to survive, to pay attention to the social world and to the high-fashion scene that was suddenly becoming important.

We were the ones to recognize designers as designers and as "stars." We had started covering designers' every move—where they lived, what they ate, how they dressed, who they saw. Humanizing them was not difficult, because for the most part they are such lively subjects. By now an important group of social women who in days gone by had hidden from publicity were seen everywhere, and we started photographing them at restaurants and even at private parties. These women were beginning to accept the top designers in their homes. We had interviewed Babe Paley and Gloria Guinness, and I was impressed when the Duchess of Windsor asked to meet me. But my father had warned me, as he sat at his rolltop desk, which had belonged to his father E. W., the founder of Fairchild, "Don't start believing your own publicity."

At that time I thought the Duchess of Windsor was one of the chicest women I had ever met—charming and witty. Today a bit wiser, I hope, and more cynical, I know, I realize that the life of the Duchess and her King was a total waste: dressing up for lunch and dinner—the Duchess paying practically nothing for her clothes—going to balls, sailing on the S.S. *United States,* not even paying any fare, sort of "renting themselves out" for an evening, redecorating their Waldorf-Astoria suite on each visit to the United States. The Windsor story went on and on and they just faded away. About the only romantic memories left of them are in books, and the only symbol of the Windsor glory is the Duchess's pearl necklace that now hangs on the neck of lovely Mrs. Calvin Klein.

All members of the governing body of my family except for Uncle Harry had been against our ideas for a new publication. Cousin Edgar had rubbed his nose and told me to go back to the third floor: the editorial floor. (Advertising people to this day at *WWD/W* are not permitted to come down to the third floor to talk to reporters or editors without permission.) "John," he said firmly, "remember we are publishers of trade papers, not consumer publications."

Yet Tom Murphy, his eyes smiling, said simply, "John, how long will it take you to do the first issue?" I couldn't respond right away, because I was so pleased. I left his office, nervous in the knowledge that in one month we had to create our first-ever consumer newspaper.

When the first tabloid dummy of *W* appeared, we almost stopped breathing. The cartoon cover was a full-color picture of Richard Nixon and Pat looking like a couple out of a Frankenstein movie. It was 1972, and the press and the intellectuals wanted to kick Nixon about, but this cover was a real mistake. And the rest of the contents weren't much better. Frank Magid of the Iowa Research Group immediately confirmed our worst thoughts. Forget it.

Up I went to Tom Murphy with the bad news. "Not too good," he said, pausing a second, then rolling his eyes as if he had come to a quick decision, added, "Try again. What have we got to lose?"

At that time Michael Coady, former head of our Chicago office, had taken over as editor of *WWD*. From the first I admired his free spirit. Michael and I settled down and came up with another approach. And with John Sias, president of the Capital Cities Publishing Division, we launched the first *W*.

Up on the ninth floor in Uncle Edgar's old office, we had a very brief meeting at which I defined what *W* should be. "Now, it's got to be big size, super big, nothing like *Vogue* or *Harper's Bazaar,* so big that everyone will see the difference. And inside we have to have the newest fashions in full color months before the fashion magazines can publish the same thing. In short, we want to produce a fashion newspaper with the speed of a newspaper, but in full color and with the smart look of a fashion magazine." Michael and John didn't say a word, so I went on: "Not only fashion but fine living, more about people than anything else."

As we were about to leave, John Sias, who did not like to spend money foolishly, asked if it was not possible to go to a smaller size: "Think of the money you would save on paper." We were out the door before he could persuade us to change our minds. But he was right. Years later, we trimmed less than half an inch off the big size and saved some money, and not one advertiser or reader knew the difference.

Michael Coady, Etta Froio, and Rudy Millendorf, the finest art director we ever had at Fairchild, worked closely on every detail of the new dummy. The front page included a beautiful color sketch done graciously and exclusively for us by Yves Saint Laurent: a sort of unisex drawing of a man and a woman wearing pants. And as soon as the dummy appeared on the third floor, we decided to make a study of what women really thought this time.

Our test was to be simple, conducted by the Harvard Business School on a very informal basis. Put a group of Boston women of different ages in a room and let them talk about *W*. We waited and hoped for the best. I worried that those intellectual and somewhat snobbish women of Boston would hardly enjoy reading our frivolous editorial material, that those smartass headlines I loved would hardly sit well with those women. "I WONDER WHOSE KISSINGER NOW" was hardly intellectual stuff and could strike the wrong chord. (Funnily enough, this very headline appeared in *Time* Magazine with the same sort of story. I never did ask Henry K. if he had seen it and knew we were responsible for the idea. But neither Nancy nor Henry gets upset by these unimportant games of the press.)

We did hear from those darling women of Harvard—and they gave us pretty good marks. Good enough to go ahead with the real publication, despite the grumbling we heard that *W* "would never fly." On the advertising floor, the sales people were clearly against the project. They were worried that *W* would cut into the business of *WWD*. And over and over again we kept hearing on the outside and inside that no one wanted still another fashion publication. To think how many fashion publications there are today and more to come.

Undaunted, we moved ahead. The first issue came out quietly: no advance publicity or advertising, no hype of any kind, only our own enthusiasm on the editorial floor and the support of "uptown" (Capital Cities) propelled us forward.

I retreated to the isle of Bermuda and waited. Nothing happened, except for a call from Dan Burke, president of Capital Cities. Dan had received the first issue of *W* and he "wanted to thank me." I waited for him to make some comment, but he did not. I think like everyone else he wanted to wait and see if we could keep going on a twice-a-month basis. I suspect he was not impressed, nor were others sitting up top. I stared out to sea—searching for self-confidence as the blue-green waves broke gently over the coral reefs.

Back in New York there was still no reaction, but there was no time for us to be depressed, because we were so busy doing the second issue.

Then we got one big break.

We were dining (black tie) with Charles and Lyn Revson for the first time in their Park Avenue apartment, which in its day was one of the largest in New York. Dinner for the eight of us was in the library—the dining room was reserved for twenty-five or more—and I was seated next to Lyn. Behind every chair was a footman. The sommelier kept filling up my glass with Haut Brion 1955.

From the other end of the table Revson interrupted the conversation: "Fairchild, that paper called *W*, I got it the other day. I like the size. I'm signing up for a full page every issue. You know why? Because it is like a billboard, a giant billboard for Revlon."

True to his word Revlon was our first big advertiser, securing a preferred position, and they launched their new perfume, Charlie, in *W*.

Still, for three years we got little reaction to *W*. Sometimes I wondered whether the newspaper was even being delivered. The orders for advertising space were hardly pouring in.

Once in a while, we editorial animals have to face reality. If no one takes advertising in your publication, you might as well fold it quickly. You can't assume that if a publication is really good the advertisers will have to advertise.

So Michael went hustling for all he was worth, and I knew I had better hustle too. Leonard and Evelyn Lauder of Estée Lauder invited me to dinner in Banksville to discuss *W*. Leonard was not enthusiastic about the big size and Evelyn asked why we needed another fashion publication. To answer Evelyn, I said, "*W* is unique in that we publish fashion three to six months before *Vogue* and *Harper's Bazaar*." I added, "Fashion is news as it happens. There is nothing worse than looking at old clothes hanging in the stores on markdown racks. By the time the magazines are out, the top designers are already making new clothes." I was warming up, and Evelyn and Leonard could see that I was enthusiastic. "And besides," I continued, "*W* is not just about fashion but about life style, fine living, and people." They just listened politely, and as we went back to New York in their limousine, I was sure they had decided to wait and see. Rightfully so.

We commissioned another study from Frank Magid of Des Moines, Iowa. The new study was neither good nor bad, but neutral. One section said that the readers of *W* did not like gossip. But several pages later the study said readers liked the "EYE" column, which certainly bordered on gossip.

Michael Coady, who sits right across from me at the office, was reading these lines when he got up from his desk, took the report, and thumped it into the wastepaper basket. Just then John Sias, who had commissioned the Magid report, arrived at our desks, and asked if we had seen the study. When he saw it in the wastepaper basket right in front of him, he looked at both of us and shook his head, but we never discussed the study again.

To capture the imagination of the reader we experimented with many ideas, but held to our determination to surprise our reader in every issue. We were not going to be like anything else out there. Fortunately, we had a wonderful slice of life to choose from, and our readers were constantly in search of fun and excitement in the new era of plenty and greed. The timing for us was perfect. Americans like new ideas and new ways to enjoy life. That's the strength of the U.S.A.: we are positive thinkers and we are always prepared to go in a new direction. Americans accept the new fashions way ahead of the Europeans, especially the French, who are the last to accept even the ideas that come directly from them.

For three years, we plodded along—and looking back I would say that in a way we performed a publishing miracle —at least some of our competitors have told me so. A miracle because the production costs on *W* are high. The big size eats up lots of paper every issue. Our excellent color reproduction is achieved at great expense.

Then slowly but surely we started getting advertising and reader reaction. You know you have made it with a new publication when you hear people say, "I read that piece. It was amusing." Or "I read about him in *W*." We saw *The New York Times Magazine* copy our layout. Neiman Marcus and other stores copied our layouts and ideas in their own store magazines. In Hong Kong, the Chinese produced our style in an even bigger size. We watched our circulation grow steadily and after careful analysis decided to keep it at 275,000, with one of the highest media incomes in the industry. But we were stuck with a tough problem: to keep the circulation small and still keep our advertising rates high. We managed because we were supported in advertising by the fashion establishment. Not Seventh Avenue—the top American designers except for Calvin Klein and Ralph Lauren have never been big advertisers—but the top European designers: Armani, Valentino, and then the French. Still, without the support of the cosmetics industry, it would be extremely difficult today for any top publication to survive. Revson and the Lauders helped make *W* possible.

Creative editors are hard to find, and to be creative they cannot spend their time bogged down in the bureaucracy of publishing—cost controls, budgeting, printing, circulation, advertising. A good editor has to spend his time getting out of his office to find out what his reader is thinking. Never ask readers what they want to read, because basically they don't know until they have a magazine or newspaper article in front of them. Then they can tell you what they like or don't like. One thing is certain: they don't want to be bored with long-winded, detailed pieces without any interpretation.

We have fine editors who work together as a team. Our

office is informal, so that we can all see each other and work up good and bad ideas.

Across from me and next to me are Patrick McCarthy and Jane Lane, the two best creative editors I know. There they are now, huddled over the computer, Patrick tapping away with a Cheshire-cat smile, Jane, looking at the screen, and suddenly laughing raucously. They love the lines that they have just written. That's the real name of the publishing game: words pouring out with real gusto. As I watch Patrick and Jane creating the cover story on the Invisible People, I sense that we are onto a "hot story." But only our precious reader will decide. That's the story in publishing and in fashion.

And we do have fun along the way, even though covering social events, the comings and the goings of society, can stretch the patience and imagination. To say what really happened is another matter, but we do—up to a point—tell the truth about a big evening when the women dress to be seen and photographed. We send our own special reporter, the Countess Louise J. Esterhazy, who has a sharp eye and a sting in her writing. She rarely misses a trick.

Come with her to a charity evening at the Paris Opera to see how High Society, International Style, behaves when suddenly confronted by a French strike.

First some background. Baroness Marie-Hélène de Rothschild, who once reigned as sort of a social queen of Tout Paris, decided reluctantly to organize the event: a special première performance of Rudolf Nureyev's newly choreographed "Sleeping Beauty." She should have refused. Two days before, the Baroness, who neither gives up nor forgives, was informed at her residence, the Hôtel Lambert on the Île Saint-Louis, that the Paris Opera Ballet dancers might call a strike even though the evening's proceeds were for them.

Our Countess Louise Esterhazy arrived early the night of the party with her pen and paper. The Baroness de Roths-

child was in a high state. She kept saying, "Let me talk to
the union; they will dance for me." Behind her back the
directors of the Opera turned pale. "Don't let her near
them," whispered one of them. Meanwhile, down below in
the cellar of the Opera, a Communist official hid the keys to
the entrance of the main auditorium. When the keys could
not be found, Marie-Hélène fainted. Already the guests
were outside pushing at the doors to get in. Hot on the story,
Louise, dressed in a draped black-and-white Cardin dress
(she had a large black-and-white feather in her white hair),
climbed up and down the grand staircase, scribbling notes
in her pad. Here is some of what she reported to *WWD/W*
that Friday evening:

> Marie-Hélène's day had begun ominously. As La Baronne
> took her Fauchon tea at the Hôtel Lambert, Princess Caro-
> line called from Saint Moritz to say she was fogbound and
> would not attend the ballet gala. A frantic Marie-Hélène
> rang Karl Lagerfeld amid all the excitement of his fashion
> show to verify the princess's excuse. Little did she know at
> that point that this would be a minor setback compared with
> the rest of the evening.
>
> . . . As guests began to arrive, cries of "Quel scandale!"
> resounded when word spread there was to be no ballet.
> Alexis de Redé pleaded continually, "Calme, du calme."
> Pierre Bergé, strutting like a cock, ran to Marie-Hélène's
> side as she stood stoically—and spotlighted—at the top of
> the grand staircase, greeting each of her guests.
>
> Meanwhile, a thirsty crowd wandered through Jean-
> François Daigre's bow-laden balconies in a desperate
> search for champagne. Former budget minister Alain Juppé
> couldn't find a glass so he drank directly from the bottle of
> Veuve Clicquot rosé 1979 with a straw. One exasperated
> American grabbed a bottle and served the guests himself. A
> few Nouvelle aristos sarcastically shouted: "Vive les social-
> istes!"
>
> "This evening is like the Marx brothers in Fellini's *Night
> at the Opera,*" observed one Paris couturier. . . .

Bitchery reigned. Lady D. looked around the room and sniffed, "This looks like an assemblage of overdressed women at Grand Central Station en route to Tarrytown." Countess B., wearing a sable-trimmed stole made by Oscar de la Renta in a fabric André Oliver had discovered, surveyed the first-floor grand foyer, where VIPs sat behind a golden arch while the peasants dined in the hallway. "This room is hideous to begin with," she said. "And all this funereal gold wrapping only makes it look worse." The room would have been glitzier still if firemen had not pulled down the sparkling gold curtains just before dinner began because they had not been fireproofed.

The décor in the grand entrance, which simulated a fairytale woods with real sleeping beauties lying amid the trees, was as spectacular as the fashion extravaganza of clothes the ladies of Paris wore. But most of the women just couldn't carry their dresses off. Like the fairytale of "Sleeping Beauty" itself, where a spell is cast and the entire castle falls asleep, the evening was one big snooze. But there were no Prince Charmings to wake them up.

6

NOUVELLE SOCIETY AND THE OLD GUARD

asically, designers design for—and depend on— wealthy clients linked together in a solid-gold chain that stretches across countries and continents, people infused with a combination of money and power that gives them rights and privileges almost beyond the comprehension of the unlinked —people like you and me. I never cease to be amazed at them; not impressed, just amazed.

Collectively, they constitute a society of material luxury that is impoverished in its relations with just about everybody else, often even with those who are part of the same chain. They are so busy going places—the "right" places, of course—seeing and being seen with the "right" people with the most money, that they have precious little time for normal, everyday, banal routine. Sometimes—no, often—they forget that the rest of the world is living another way.

I find myself intrigued at their comings and goings, the extravagant lives they live. I suppose that is because I speak from inside this special world, and sometimes I catch myself falling into the same pit of emptiness. Most of the chain hate to be alone, and when trapped without a luncheon, a dinner, or a vacation with the rest of the pack, they are sure they have fallen from grace, or worse, that they are Out. (More of *W*'s notorious Ins and Outs lists later.)

Picture the scene: a rainy Monday morning, yet another cover to think up for *W*, and all I'm drawing is a great big blank. Nobody seems to be in a fashion-cover mood. There sit the troika—editors Etta Froio and Patrick McCarthy and copublisher Michael Coady—on the red glazed-chintz couch in my office. I am sprawled on a black cane chair, leaning on the shiny black marble table I use for a desk. The only thing I'm sure of is that I've got to get a haircut.

"You know," I begin, "there's been a big change in society; today it's all money and power and greed." The words trail off, but at least nobody disagrees. I'm sounding like a lecture, I think, but I push on anyway. "We have to give this society a name that means something to the reader. Not 'nouveau riche; but 'nouveau' something. We've got nouvelle cuisine, we've got nouvelle . . . That's it! Nouvelle Society."

And so another addition to our fashion glossary was hatched—a list that includes "hot pants" (it's in the new Webster's dictionary); "tough chic"; "sportive"; "longuette" (forgot that one: a big mistake); "Her Elegance" (for Jacqueline Kennedy Onassis); "Her Drear" (for Princess Margaret); "Fashion Victim" (for the expensively misguided); and "Social Cyclone" (a generic label for such as

Ivana Trump, Georgette Mosbacher, Anne Bass, Mercedes [ex-Kellogg] Bass, et al.) My personal favorites are "Walkers" (the single men who escort the Social Cyclones to parties that their husbands don't want to go to), and "Social Moth," reserved exclusively for Harlem landlord Jerome Zipkin, the Walker of Walkers.

It wasn't long before the term "Nouvelle Society" caught on, and before we knew it, people were secretly—and not so secretly—labeling their friends. It's moments like these that make it all worthwhile.

I'll wager that "Nouvelle Society" will make the dictionaries too, or at least become part of the social history of the greedy '80s. For, looking back, today's Old Society were once Nouvelles themselves, prepared to pay any price and devote all their energies to greedily conquering the rest of us. Now, inbred and incapable of throwing parties on the scale of today's Nouvelles, the Old Guard disparage the Nouvelles behind their backs but never turn down one of their invitations.

How best to describe Nouvelle Society? In the words of Aileen Mehle, who writes under the name Suzy in the New York *Post* and other newspapers, "It's dreadful that money is God"—but you must have money, lots of it, to break into the wonderful world of Nouvelle. Charm certainly doesn't hurt, and it might put you ahead of the pack for a time, but the money is essential, for Nouvelle Society does not believe in a no-frills way of life.

For example, few batted an eyelash when Si Newhouse, of the Condé Nast empire, paid $17 million for Jasper Johns's painting "False Start." And Robert Bass, Sid's investment tycoon brother, paid $12 million for an Early American secretary, of which there are only four others in existence. Such art belongs in a museum, but fewer and fewer pieces of real quality are getting there, because of Nouvelle Society's zeal for hanging masterpieces on their own walls whenever possible. The Nouvelles are forever playing a form of Monopoly in the painting, fine art, and antiques market, and there seems to be no end to their insatiable appetite to acquire and show off their precious— and sky-high expensive—possessions. (Case in point: Gayfryd Steinberg, a Nouvelle beauty if there ever was one, presides over a thirty-four-room apartment so filled with Titians and Rodins that she had to hire a curator from the Metropolitan Museum to catalog them all.)

Elaborate decorations and period furniture in gargantuan apartments, regal entertaining with flowers flown in from England, travel by private jet or on the Concorde, and couture clothes at prices high enough to build a small summer cottage are the trappings of Nouvelle Society.

When Nouvelles eat, it's a formal affair. Petrus, one of the most expensive of the French Bordeaux, flows like water, and the caviar is heaped up. Banker Edmond Safra and his wife, Lily, served so much caviar at one of their dinners that a guest—who shall remain nameless—dispensed with the toast points altogether and called for a spoon, to go after double helpings of the "Iranian gold." At leavetaking, each guest was presented with an exquisite ivory picture frame.

I well remember a hot night outside Rome in the company of the Safras. Lily had just finished buying her wardrobe for the season from Valentino, and the designer had asked the three of us and a few other friends to dinner at his palazzo on the Appian Way. After passing through tall, electronically controlled gates at the front entrance, we moved into Valentino's garden, something straight out of *Ben Hur,* with the grass a dazzling emerald green and every plant bathed in light. There was a pool grand enough for an Esther Williams production number, and the palazzo, its already perfect lines enhanced by Italian Nouvelle Society decorator Mongiardino, would have made a Caesar smile. Yet across the road from Valentino's palazzo is a hamburger stand!

I was seated next to Mr. Safra, and I suppose that like everybody who finds himself in the company of a banking giant, I was hoping for a hot tip.

"What's going on in the financial world?" I asked. He looked at me, his dark eyes, under his even darker eyebrows, clearly indicating that my dumb question was not being well received. Then, realizing how stupidly persistent I was likely to be, he summed up his world view. "When I give Lily a dollar, Lily spends two dollars." He put a large forkful of green noodles into his mouth. "That's our one big problem in the world today," he concluded. "We're all spending money we don't really have."

Dinner over, we headed back to Rome, while our host, because of kidnapping threats, passed through five separate doors on his way to bed, locking each one with a different key before turning out the lights. After her fittings were over, Lily would head back to New York—"my favorite place," she confided. "It is the capital of the world." Maybe; what it is, most definitely, is the capital of Nouvelle Society.

The idea of Nouvelle Society took almost nine months to truly catch on, but soon *WWD/W* was chronicling the comings and goings of the billionaire John Kluges, Trumps, Gettys, Basses, Kravises, Taubmans, Steinbergs, and others not quite as rich but more than eager to spend their way into Nouvelledom. The money wasn't the question; the real question was whether society—the Old Guard—would embrace the Nouvelles, richer by billions and vastly more aggressive than the Wobbly Wasp establishment.

But speaking of society, I asked a well-known and most-civilized Frenchman once what he would call a civilized woman. He answered, "Naturellement, elle est une grande dame." But calling her a great lady makes her sound heavy, too big. The woman I have in mind has manners, education, and style, for sure, but also inner strength, principles, love, tolerance. She cannot be too aggressive but she must be able to defend herself from those who out of jealousy try to tear her to shreds or to take advantage of her.

Liza Minnelli came up with the term for my civilized woman—"Well, John, she is just a great dame"—and that says it for today's American fine lady.

Of all of the Old Guard, Brooke Astor is without question the Queen of New York. Even her name, Mrs. Vincent Astor, conveys a certain aura. She is respected, loved—and never boring. And she has an uncanny sense about people.

I was alone with her at La Côte Basque one day when with a gleam in her eye she asked me, "Do you think they make love often?" referring to two newly united lovers. Before I could even try to answer, the eighty-seven-year-old great dame smiled sweetly and said, "When I was young I used to fall in love all the time—and how wonderful, wonderful." Her words trailed off rather sadly and I realized she would always be in love—with life.

The Astor Foundation under her direction has given huge sums of money to many projects, but what is more important is that Brooke gets out and sees to it that the foundation money is used wisely. She and Richard Salomon, former head of Charles of the Ritz, saved the New York Public Library from death. As she told me of the roof leaking water onto precious manuscripts, she was visibly moved. It was clear she was ready to dry each and every one of those books.

At home there is another side to the Brooke Astor story. After work she enjoys giving grand dinner parties and slyly mixes her groups. Like a Marine general (her father was a Marine colonel) she takes you by the arm and says, "Come on now, you have spent enough time talking to Barbara Walters. Go talk to Bill Paley. He wants to see you." And of course you go whether you want to or not. She calls you to dinner with a big wooden-handled dinner bell she rings herself. And after dinner there are often speeches.

At one such dinner, Brooke Astor greeted Jayne Wrightsman at the door and exclaimed, "Jayne, I guess that dress
cost at least forty thousand dollars," to which Jayne replied,
"Thirty-seven thousand." For the rest of the evening, the
other guests kept their eyes on the flowered chiffon dress
by Marc Bohan, who that day had "resigned" from Christian Dior.

When the Reagans entered the White House, Brooke
Astor was the first to give a dinner party for them. When
WWD learned that Charlotte Curtis of *The New York
Times* was on the guest list but that we could not cover the
dinner, I was furious for a long time. We even avoided
photographing the Queen of New York—until one day at La
Grenouille she caught my eye and waved and made me
realize she was a much bigger person than I.

And she proved a big person when it came time to judge
Nouvelle Society.

The vivacious Brooke Astor waved her magic wand in
approval, telling *W*: "People with money and taste are always welcome." The city's two princesses, Mrs. William
(Pat) Buckley and Mrs. Samuel Pryor (Annette) Reed, also
gave their blessing. And why not? Together, these three
women raised enough money to ensure the survival of many
of New York's finest museums and the New York Public
Library. Clearly, Nouvelle Society wanted a place to go with
its money, and what could be a happier marriage? Power
and money would fuse to make New York even more the
City of Cities.

Like Brooke Astor, Pat Buckley devotes her life to charity
and to helping people. She has raised money for the Metropolitan Museum, Sloan-Kettering, St. Vincent's Hospital
AIDS care. Her name and energetic participation guarantee
a successful money-raising event.

And she can work under all kinds of conditions. Take the
time she was sitting on the floor of her duplex 778 Park
Avenue apartment (778 Park seems to be the residence of

great dames—Astor and Buckley). Pat was surrounded by large bound volumes of *W:* five years of the newspaper. In the next room a sanding machine was at work on the floor. Carpenters were laying a new parquet. The curtains in the living room were tied back off the floor. The ceilings were peeling and the whole duplex smelled of mildew mixed with varnish. Pat Buckley's crutch leaned against a sheet-covered chair. There had been a water-main break on Seventy-second Street and the flood waters had inundated the Buckley apartment. Undaunted, Mrs. B. was telling me of a telephone conversation she had just had. "Imagine that —Alex Gregory (Vendome Press) wants to eliminate articles in *W* about his Nouvelle Society friends, the Trumps and the Taubmans." Pat was in the process of editing for Gregory a book with significant articles from *W* over the years. "He's taking all the guts out of your work and I won't let him." How could you not love a lady who was defending the honor of our *W*? We decided to abandon the project with Gregory.

There was the time Pat and I were at Le Cirque. The white wine was already on the table and Pat and I were awaiting Gustav Zumsteg, the Swiss fabric manufacturer, and plotting how Pat could get from him, for free, more than two thousand yards of silk shantung for the Metropolitan Museum's Costume Institute's Party of the Year. The shy but dignified Zumsteg arrived, and I could see in his eyes that though he was impressed to be lunching with such a grand lady, his Swiss nature told him to watch out.

The more we talked and the more wine we consumed, the more uneasy Mr. Zumsteg seemed. I thought Pat would never ask for the fabric. But when she did it was in a way Zumsteg could not resist. She based it all on the fact that the evening was built around Yves Saint Laurent: "But Gustav, what an honor for Yves Saint Laurent, a whole evening for an exhibition of his work." And she thereby had the fabric almost up on the Met's walls. She knew that Gustav worshiped Saint Laurent. Zumsteg sacrificed enough of his beautiful shantung to make thousands of dresses. (When the evening was over, Pat had the fabric removed from the walls and sold it "downtown to someone," thereby putting more money in the Metropolitan's coffers. Later on, Zumsteg's shantung was seen around town on the backs of many women.)

Annette Reed was a young princess of New York society long before the days of Nouvelle, and she has blossomed on the New York scene, becoming one of the Three Muskerettes: Astor-Buckley-Reed. What the three fine ladies have in common is energy and charm that can gird people into action. Not only do they raise millions in a season but they add joy throughout the hard, brutal city. Annette can laugh uproariously even while she goes into battle on all fronts. Following in her mother, Jane Engelhard's, footsteps, she became a trustee of the Metropolitan Museum, the New York Public Library, and Rockefeller University.

Annette has been considered a wild lady ever since her days at her finishing school, Foxcroft, where she let all the horses out of the barn because she thought they should be free. She still does things by her own rules. In the hot days of August, she can be found in Katonah, New York, doing her gardening in a black bathing suit. Her swimming pool is also black. And when she takes her guests for a drive along the winding dirt roads, she has one hand on the wheel and the other on Pickles, the Cairn terrier on her lap.

Annette has a certain power over men, makes each one feel he is the only one. I've seen her make William S. Paley, CBS chairman, roar with laughter, and I've seen her inspire Henry Kissinger as well as her museum friends. She admires people who work at their jobs and she has that way of saying, "Go for it." And a big part of her life and joy is Oscar de la Renta, whom she is expected to marry soon.

· · ·

The first of the Nouvelles to make a splash were John Gut-freund and his seductive, eager wife, Susan. Their parties became legends in opulence. It was Bill Blass who brought them to our attention. "What a party last night!" he chor-tled over lunch. "Every chair was twined in roses. Beautiful, even though the thorns sometimes stuck in your back or caught the ladies' hair. Bowls of fruit like I've never seen, so fantastically arranged I was afraid to touch them. John insisted that I have a peach, but I was afraid to take one."

No one talked much about the guest list; the talk was about how Susan entertained. At that point, nobody really ridiculed them; people were just too overwhelmed that in this day and age a couple would go to all that effort and spend all that money. But the stock market was booming and Salomon Brothers was breaking out in bonds. And Susan, who occasionally offered friends colorful tales from her days as an airline stewardess, was determined to go one step further. She was going to learn all there was to know—not just about entertaining but about decorating and furniture, paintings and the French. She redid her hus-band's London office in a style so extravagant that it brought smiles to the lips of Salomon executives, many of whom would lose their shirts on Black Monday, 1987.

Susan Gutfreund's tutor in the more refined ways of life was Jayne Wrightsman, who had earlier played her own game of social climbing in Palm Beach, a town of no great refinement or distinction, in my book. It was Wrightsman, first spotted as a young "girl about town" in Beverly Hills, who, together with Mrs. Paul (Bunny) Mellon, took the young Jacqueline Kennedy under her wing in the early days of Camelot, training her in the finer collectibles of life.

I remember hearing stories of how Mellon and Wrights-man lavished gifts on the Kennedy children, including, from Mellon, a canopy bed for young Caroline. Stranded there in the cultural desert of Palm Beach, Jacqueline Kennedy, a refined woman in her own right, not surprisingly gravitated to the chic Jayne, who was married to a rich rough-and-tough businessman.

Wrightsman was very much a fine-furniture Francophile, and in Susan she had a willing pupil. For her part, Susan, who had been dressed by Givenchy even before she met Jayne, became even more skilled at embodying the Givenchy look. Before her Nouvelle party days were over, Susan fled the shores of Manhattan for Paris, where she continues to hold forth in French and Italian mixed with a touch of Texas twang.

With the encouragement of Wrightsman and Givenchy, she bought the top floor of a *hôtel particulier* on the rue de Grenelle, in the fashionable Seventh Arrondissement, the right address on the Left Bank, and decorator Henri Samuel created a charming home. Givenchy, who then, as now, had great taste in houses, soon moved into the building. On paying a visit to the Gutfreunds' *hôtel particulier,* Mrs. Deane Johnson (the ex-Mrs. Henry Ford) was duly impressed by the living quarters, but what truly excited her were the commodious parking facilities, complete with a car wash, in the basement.

The Gutfreunds now live some of the happiest moments of their lives in Paris. Over time, Susan has displayed improvement in her French, and with her still good friend, Jayne, she has persuaded the curators at Versailles to open the palace for small private showings to visiting friends. (So as not to be outdone by those who would later accompany her, she took the precaution of having M. Samuel elucidate the fine points of Versailles's great rooms beforehand.)

Known for her lavish gifts, Gutfreund bought for more than $15,000 Marie Antoinette's letters and sent them to the grandest of the Rothschilds, Liliane, who promptly mailed them back. John regularly wings his way on the Concorde to Paris, where Susan continues to give grand dinners for leading members of French society and for tycoons like Gianni Agnelli, head of Fiat, banker Michel David-Weill, and others who seldom venture out except to see Susan and John. Parisians continue to be titillated by Susan, who spares no expensive effort to give everyone a grand evening —outdoing the snobbish French at their own game and being more French than the French. She has even sent her butler to Versailles to buy string beans—"the best in France."

Susan's mentor, Jayne Wrightsman, has always intrigued me. One evening as she was wafting waves of her strong perfume (created especially for her) through the *couloirs* of the Ritz, we ran into each other. She was dressed to the nines—but no Fashion Victim—and decked out for an elegant Paris evening. I was walking Roderick, our King Charles spaniel, through the lobby, hoping that he would not stop to do his business on the thick blue Persian carpet in front of the concierge's desk. Mrs. Wrightsman stopped me and, in her soft, Locust Valley lockjaw, murmured, "Good evening, Mr. Fairchild."

Extending a very thin hand (big diamond, medium quality), she looked down regally at Roderick and observed: "How peculiar. You know, your dog has a feather in his mouth." And she walked on.

In her Palm Beach days, Jayne Wrightsman might have been considered Nouvelle Society by some. But when one of her step-daughters married Cholly Knickerbocker, the gossip columnist for the now defunct New York *Journal-American* (his real name was Igor Cassini), the whole idea of society was different. Marie-Hélène de Rothschild remembers telling friends while on her honeymoon with Baron Guy that she intended to stay with the Wrightsmans in Palm Beach. "My friends kept telling me that it just wasn't the right thing to do," she said, but the Baroness went anyway, and she never told me whether she enjoyed herself or not. She only laughed, saying, "The world turns."

Those were the days in Palm Beach when the Kennedys reigned supreme. But truth be told, before the Kennedys

achieved the White House, they were not accepted with
open arms by all of Palm Beach—probaby because there
were just too many rich Republicans against them. The
Kennedys had lots of teeth and lots of money, but they were
never really embraced by the Old Guard.

But when Jackie moved into the White House, she transformed it, with the help of Bunny Mellon and Jayne
Wrightsman, into her idea of an elegant palace. Jackie en-
gaged a French chef, and even the kitchen turned sophisticated. The Rose Garden, planted by Bunny, made the social
headlines. The Jackie Kennedy era made formal entertaining de rigueur, and even Wobbly Wasps clamored to be
invited to what the French were grudgingly calling the
"Maison Blanche."

I include this trivia about Jayne Wrightsman and Jacqueline Kennedy Onassis only because their influence gets to
the taproot of what we've come to call Nouvelle Society. As
old met new, and a drab, boring White House rose to new
heights of social popularity, everybody wanted to be invited.
Was that power or was that money? The politics didn't
change, but the style did. President Kennedy was right
when he said that the world seemed to be more interested
in what Jackie was wearing than in the serious events of the
day. Frivolous? Perhaps, but Americans and the rest of the
world have always had a thing about glamour and the romantic idea that the rich and powerful have something special to offer. As a result, the general public has a seemingly
unquenchable thirst for news about the lavish and greedy
ways of Nouvelle Society.

Jackie invented the idea of American royalty with the
help of her court, and she still knows how to find the best
of everything through the help of her friends—especially of
old friends like Bunny Mellon, who, in her own quiet way,
passes the time creating beautiful gardens and amassing a
superb botanical library in Upperville, Virginia.

Bunny is a perfectionist and has been known to take on

young painters, who work for years on the floors and walls of her houses in New York, Cape Cod, and Antigua. Her floors are painted with shadows, so that on a dreary day the sunlight still seems to be streaming through. Her vegetable garden is laid out on the bias, and her gardening clothes are designed by Givenchy himself.

Not to be forgotten is her Waspy, Anglophile husband, Paul, one of America's finest art collectors and philanthropists, his largesse dispensed with grace. What a contrast to the new breed of Nouvelles, who donate willingly but require a speedy return on their charitable investments. Respectability, social recognition, and power are now the watchwords. A seat on the board of the Metropolitan Museum is worth as much as any leveraged buyout. In fact, Henry Kravis, the King of the Leveraged Buyout, donated $10 million to the Met before he got his board seat.

The Astors made a fortune in fur trading, the Vanderbilts in railroads, the Rockefellers in oil and real estate, and the Kennedys in bootleg Scotch whisky. So what's different about today's Nouvelle Society, obsessed with buyouts, takeovers, stocks, bonds, and mergers? Simple. It's the money. The aspirations of Nouvelle Society have moved on to a lavishness beyond most people's richest dreams.

Brooke Astor is right when she says: "In my day, a million was a lot. Today a billion is more like it."

Mrs. Astor is not the only one overwhelmed by the new wealth, and it did not take long before the press began tracking the comings and goings of Nouvelle Society. Occasional members of the Fourth Estate themselves were accepted into the same rich group, though they could hardly lay claim to great family fortunes. *W* hit the newsstands in December 1987 with its first issue on the Nouvelles, and in an offbeat accident of timing, television commentator Barbara Walters, Ann Getty (husband Gordon's fortune is estimated at more than $1 billion), Anne Bass, Calvin and Kelly Klein, designer Carolyne Roehm and her husband,

Henry Kravis, and Ivana Trump all became stars of the Metropolitan Museum's Costume Institute gala—a relatively sedate charity, which in the past had drawn its support from a completely different slice of society.

Barbara Walters, known for her scoops and for getting world leaders and star politicians to appear before her camera, had recently married Hollywood tycoon Merv Adelson, after many years of "dating" others, including Alan Greenspan, who became head of the Federal Reserve Bank. Immediately the Adelsons entered into Nouvelle Society and began looking for the "right" apartment. In short order, Barbara and Renata Adler of *The New Yorker,* who arrived at dinner parties in a gray pigtail and dressed like a Bryn Mawr professor, became the new doyennes of Nouvelle, and the Kissingers and Mrs. Astor began showing up on *their* guest lists.

And Walters and Adler were not the only scribes to crack the rarefied ranks of Nouvelle. The late Charlotte Curtis and the late Eugenia Sheppard, among others, happily began to mix printer's ink and after-hours pleasure at society's top tables.

Sometimes it proved difficult for a reporter to be both guest and truthful chronicler of high-powered friends. Suzy has probably managed better than just about anybody else to be a member of the social set and, at the same time, tell its real story. By dint of charm, connections, and hard work, she seems to get the scoop on the most newsworthy marriages and divorces before anyone else. Case in point: When Sid Bass ran off with Mercedes Kellogg, Suzy was first with the news, well before Bass's hometown newspaper, the Fort Worth *Star-Telegram,* woke up to the story.

While we're talking about inner circles, I should mention that the press has its inner circle too, presided over by dress manufacturer Mollie Parnis. Parnis, the Brooke Astor of the press, gathers her flock in her apartment on Sunday nights. She not only knows what is going on at the *Times,* sometimes before their editors do, but functions like a combination Ann Landers and Dr. Ruth for her coterie, advising them on their personal lives—including affairs and divorces.

On most Sundays, Media Queen Mollie assembles in her living room the likes of Dan Rather, Barbara Walters, the Henry Grunwalds (before he became our ambassador to Austria), the Mike Wallaces (Parnis presided over their subsequent divorce), the Tom Brokaws (she owns a toy store), and *New York Times* publisher Punch Sulzberger and his wife, Carol. On the evening that Laurence Tisch took over CBS, Parnis—believe it or not—had every one of those media superstars under her roof, plus CBS's founder and chairman, William Paley.

In the summer, Mollie's gang decamps to Martha's Vineyard, and Mollie, who is eighty and counting, goes right along with them. She customarily arrives with the Washington contingent, which includes the powerful Kay Graham and humorist Art Buchwald. For even there, the media royalty continue to wine and dine one another. Recently, Graham pulled off the social coup of the season by having Jackie Onassis and Nancy Reagan together at the same table.

What do we at *W* do about events like these? We cover every party as carefully as possible. In the old days, it was difficult for our editors and reporters to find out what was happening on a given night in that closed-off social world. But thanks to Nouvelle Society, our life has become easier. Too easy sometimes, because on a given night during "the season" there can be as many as fifteen events for us to cover.

The big change is, as we have seen, that Nouvelle Society *wants* them covered. It's not enough that these people have trouble spending all their new money; they seem to have an insatiable desire for publicity about how they go about trying. Many of them hire public-relations firms to "package their image." Long gone are the days when it was the Wasp prayer to have one's name in the paper three times in a lifetime: birth, marriage, and a tasteful obit.

Yet there is a limit to the amount of notoriety that even a Nouvelle can sit still for. It seems that Henry Kravis—who, in the words of his press agent, was "stressed out" following his $20 billion buyout of Nabisco—attacked Billy Norwich, the elfin society columnist of the *Daily News,* at a recent Literary Lions dinner at the New York Public Library. The previous year, Oscar de la Renta had threatened Norwich, but now Kravis, borrowing a torture technique from the Italian Red Brigades, declared that he would shoot Billy in the knees if he didn't stop writing nasty items about him and his beautiful wife, Carolyne. Fortunately, Brooke Astor strolled over and, without even knowing what had been going on, calmed the waters. The Nouvelles can buy almost anything in the world, but they have yet to control the press.

That said, they have certainly become adept at using the press to their own ends. Case in point: Felix Rohatyn, who has made millions for Lazard Frères in mergers and buyouts, had the temerity to attack the Nouvelle social calendar as wrongheaded and wasteful. Why not forget the dressing up, the wining, the dining, and the flowers, he suggested, and just give directly to the charity involved?

This time the man credited with almost single-handedly saving New York City from financial disaster had hit a raw nerve. Imagine criticizing not only the Nouvelles but society itself, worthies who for years had worked hard to raise millions for New York's fairest charities! The howls that went up pierced board room walls and fractured friendships, and Felix's wife, Liz, was forced to joust verbally with one of the princesses of New York in the middle of Seventy-second Street, in defense of her husband's inflammatory musings.

Unfortunately for Liz, the press tracked her down at a

special fitting at Bill Blass's for a charity event that very evening—she has quite a nice figure—before the storm blew out to sea. The Rohatyns continued to appear at the multiple affairs they had so severely criticized. To help quiet the winds, they made a sizable donation to the New York Public Library, the favorite charity of Queen Brooke, who never batted an eyelash.

7
A TABLE
FOR TWO

A t Le Cirque, the restaurant citadel of Nouvelle Society, Sirio Maccioni arrives early to plan the seating for the day's luncheon. The tables are packed closely together on the right side as you enter (the "right" place to sit), so that everyone will be able to follow several conversations at once.

Le Cirque will go down in history as the restaurant of the Reagan Era, and it is still the haunt of Jerome Zipkin, confidant of Nancy Reagan and of other Nouvelle ladies. In a way, he was Nancy's bridge to the outside world, the tale-bearer to one isolated in the White House or in the secured wilderness of Camp David. (Though when she called him in Connecticut once to wish him "Happy Thanksgiving," Zipkin, who was napping, ordered: "Tell her to call me back in two hours.")

As the Walker of Walkers, Zipkin has time for the rest of his flock as well. He is not loath to tell tall and pinched-in Betsy Bloomingdale (California Nouvelle) whether she is looking great or not, and if not, what she should wear and where she can get it.

Most days, Zipkin sits imperiously in the middle of the dining room, surrounded by his court of Nouvelles. At one such lunch, his attention was largely devoted to Aline Romanones, who lived in Spain for many years and had just written her account of the days "when I was a spy." During the Reagan Era, Zipkin always made sure that she was invited to the White House when the King of Spain paid a state visit.

Zipkin is also not above playing nasty, behind-the-scenes games in the world of diplomacy. He is said, for example, to have urged the Reagans to remove Thomas Enders from his post as ambassador to Spain. Why? Because he didn't think that Aline Romanones was treated properly by Tom and Gaetana Enders. And so, even though the Enderses were great favorites of the Spanish monarch, they were duly recalled to New York—where they were heartily welcomed by Zipkin.

He never seems to stop whispering conspiratorially to his ladies. Occasionally he darts sidelong glances to the side as he recognizes friends and enemies in the room.

Zipkin may be the most recognizable of the Walkers in Nouvelle Society, but he hardly invented the role. Society itself invented the Walker, specifically for the woman who, in spite of her wealth, finds herself lonely, with only a boring husband for company. Enter the Walkers, who can gossip, amuse, and advise on almost any subject under the sun, including how to entertain, whom to have for dinner, and the latest word on the latest fashions. They have even been known to provide hot tips on the stock market.

Alecko Papamarkou, another star Walker, not only walks Ann Getty but knows how to cut a deal along the way. So many deals, in fact, that the *Wall Street Journal* has profiled him on its front page.

There are numerous Walkers walking through the lives of the Nouvelles. Zipkin is considered number one because of his former close connections with the White House (in television replays of old Republican national conventions, you can see Zipkin sitting directly behind the Reagans), but now that there is a new administration in Washington, it remains to be seen whether Humpty Dumpty will continue to sit in the place of honor at Le Cirque. Even if there is a great fall, there seems little doubt but that Jerry's girls will be able to put him back together again.

Time never stands still for a super-Walker like Zipkin, who weaves his way in and among the Savage Set. Now that the Reagans have ridden off into the sunset, he is on the lookout for new spheres of influence. Today, at Le Cirque, he has lit on Ivana Trump, whose husband, Donald, is worth between $1.5 and $2 billion—depending on whether you read *Forbes* or *Fortune.* Zipkin is oozing charm, and Ivana, a recent addition to Nouvelle Society, who roared into town like a Social Cyclone, in the words of *W,* seems quite content to be sitting at center stage with the Social Moth himself.

The Trumps—especially Donald—have received more publicity than any other couple, including the Carolyne Roehm–Henry Kravis duo, to have made it in Nouvelle Society. The walls of Trump's office in his palatial tower high above Fifth Avenue display multiple images of Donald as a gorgeous "cover boy," smiling out from framed magazine covers, and the tall Ivana, reputed to have been a Czech ski champion, beams in the company of Roehm, the leading career girl of the Nouvelle world.

Ivana helicopters daily to the Trump hotels in Atlantic City to oversee the nongambling, hotel side of the Trump enterprise. Just recently, the Trumps, together, took over the historic Plaza Hotel, which Ivana is in the process of transforming into what she predicts will be New York's finest.

Whether or not Ivana will succeed at this endeavor, other hotels, as far away as Paris, have been locking up their staffs for fear that she will spirit them away. So far she has lured the head housekeeper of the Hotel Pierre to her new digs, as well as the good-looking night manager of the Carlyle. Reportedly, she saw a picture in *W* of Charles, the tallest headwaiter in town, serving Dover sole at the Carlyle and decided he simply had to be her headwaiter. He stayed at the Plaza for two months and went back to the Carlyle.

Yet there she sits serenely at Le Cirque, in a bright-red jersey dress, around her waist a wide leather belt with a brass tiger's claw dangling from it, rubbing against Zipkin, who, by the look of it, is far from displeased to have the newest star of New York all to himself.

Ivana, with her Slavic charm, has impressed the national press with her frankness. She doesn't appreciate being compared to Mrs. Helmsley, but she needn't worry. She doesn't yell or command the Plaza staff, she simply charms them. But when a member of the staff, as a joke, circulated a notice to the effect that the Trumps were offering every employee a Thanksgiving turkey, Ivana tore through the offices to find out who had written the bogus memo. Examining every printout as closely as Sherlock Holmes would have done, she found the culprit and promptly fired him, but then gave a free turkey to each employee anyway. Smart? You'd better believe it.

I had occasion to observe the Trumps in action at the U.S.

Open tennis finals last year. When they entered the Flushing Meadows stadium, every camera swung around, including those of CBS, who were covering the on-court play. I was sitting outside, having a drink under the tent, when I looked up and there on the large screen were the Trumps, looking every inch like royalty. Before the Lendl-Wilander match began, Donald stood up and signed autographs, while Ivana, accompanied by her bodyguard, sat smiling and adjusting her hair and pulling her skirt down over her knees. Both were completely aware that they had become the stars of the event. As I recall, they barely spoke to one another all afternoon.

At home high above Manhattan, the Trumps live in a private tower equal to the palace of a Caesar.

The Marquis de Goulaine and I visit Donald Trump in his office to discuss putting a "Butterfly House" in the lobby of Trump tower, so that people entering the building can enjoy seeing all kinds of butterflies. Trump passes his battery of secretaries, opens the glass door, and with his typical Trumpy charm, graciously ushers us into his office, introducing me along the way as "The Legend." (Six months later, when I was having lunch with John Taylor, the brilliant writer of *New York* Magazine, he told me Trump had introduced him as a "legend" too. But when at a party on the *Trump Princess,* Taylor approached Trump to say hello. "He didn't even remember me," Taylor said.) Spread out on a large table are drawings of his newest yacht, Italian designed, and much bigger than the old *Trump Princess.*

"Isn't she a beauty?" he says about his newest toy. "I don't know why I am building another one. I have been on the *Princess* only a few days this year. I have sold her to the Japanese for a big profit."

We talk butterflies and Trump says he will discuss the idea again in a few months. Then we are off to Trump's private quarters, escorted by two bodyguards through a secret passage. We find ourselves standing in front of two heavily embossed gold doors, large enough for his stretch limousine to go through. Trump uses all his force to unlock the doors. Before us is a panoramic view of Manhattan. The room, including the floor, is all marble and alabaster, and there are gold-filigreed, fluted marble columns. Above, painted cupids fly through a painted sky. On the left of the room, against the wall, is a fountain large enough for a small square in Paris. Trump goes to a black panel, pushes four buttons, and water spurts into the fountain from all directions, falling into its marble basin. In a corner of the room is a bar with Louis XVI chairs, the legs of which have been elongated to raise the seats to the proper level. The dining room has a marble table that can seat seventy-five people.

Trump tells us, "I just had to build these rooms to show that this fine workmanship could be done today." The workmanship is Italian. The French marquis stands stunned. He, who owns a château in Nantes with three hectares of roof, has never seen anything like Trump's palace. He tells Donald, "It must have taken a mountain of marble to build these rooms."

Let's drop in with the Trumps to a typical Nouvelle event away from the tower. Donald Trump stands next to Robert Silvers, the editor of *The New York Review of Books.* Like any good editor, Silvers has an insatiable curiosity about the rich. "Who is that man?" Donald asks Bob. Silvers tells him it is John Richardson, who has just completed the first volume of the definitive biography of Picasso. "Oh," says Donald, as he moves in on Richardson, and within minutes he is shaking Richardson by the hand, declaring, "Nice to meet you at last. Now I won't have to read any book on Picasso except yours." Richardson beams and thinks Trump is a splendid fellow.

Not necessarily by choice, Richardson has himself ended up being a Walker to New York's Nouvelle élite. His wicked, sandpaper tongue titillates the likes of Annette Reed, Pat Buckley, and Brooke Astor—the royals. He also has one of the best eyes around for paintings and other fine objects, expertly learned at the Wildenstein gallery and from the days when he lived with the great art collector Douglas Cooper.

Putting this knowledge and his great eye to work, Richardson helps Reed—who has a sharp eye and tongue of her own—and others buy the finest paintings, antiques, and *objets luxe* favored by the wealthy.

Another favorite of the Ladies Who Lunch is Ashton Hawkins, executive vice-president of the Met, who walks Brooke Astor with great pleasure as far away as the Park Hotel in Baden-Baden, Germany. Hawkins, who resembles a tall wild Cossack, also keeps the women of the Met board laughing as they regularly sweeten the Museum's already sizable endowment.

To the husbands of the Nouvelles, Walkers are totally acceptable, and to the women, a good Walker is probably as good as having a lover. *W* not only invented the term "Walker" for these gentlemen, but makes it a point to photograph and interview them regularly, because they know what is going on virtually every second of every day and every night. Walkers are flown to faraway places and to the country homes of ladies to provide entertainment and to charm the hostesses and their guests.

Walkers make for great stories. They are every bit as competitive as the women they escort. They are extremely careful whom they walk and where. Who pays the bills for the Walkers—the women being walked, their husbands, or the Walkers themselves? Nosy as we are, we tried once to find out if Mr. Zipkin pays for all his ladies. The only answer we got from Sirio was a wink.

We're told that Nancy Reagan used to get *WWD* by special messenger and that when she spotted new faces running across our pages, they would often turn up at White House parties. More often than not, the Nouvelles were out in force at the Reagan White House, where the guest lists were seldom laced with a very intellectual crowd.

In the Reagan age of plenty, the White House staff went to great lengths to make an evening memorable. The Reagans regularly went beyond the call of duty, and they seemed genuinely to enjoy every ostentatious moment of it.

One night stands out with particular clarity. It was a state dinner for the Sultan of Oman, and the White House never looked more lovely. Huge potted trees were everywhere, and the members of the Sultan's all-male court, turbaned and with their daggers hanging by their sides, stood behind each chair. In the middle of dinner, Mrs. Reagan's secretary approached my table and asked me to come afterward to the Blue Room. Such an invitation does a lot for the ego, no matter who you are. I went, and there was Mrs. Reagan waiting for me, all in red and looking extremely fragile. She held out her hands and then drew me to her and kissed me. I suddenly realized how delicate she was, though the press had said over and over that she needed no protection and was indeed the world's best protector of the President.

Calvin Klein interrupted our meeting, ending my brief encounter with the First Lady after only a few words of personal greeting. Sadly, it has been three years since I've seen Nancy Reagan, three years since that Blue Room embrace—though she did have her secretary call our Washington office one day and ask why Jerry Zipkin's face had been cropped out of a picture taken at a White House party. Thereafter, Zipkin, the Walker of Walkers, was not seen quite as often at Mrs. Reagan's side.

But I digress. To see Nouvelle Society in action costs only the price of a luncheon at Le Cirque. It's expensive, but the food is good, especially the pasta primavera and the Italian white truffles when they're in season, but when you go, be sure you are not stuck away to the side, or with your back up against the left-hand wall. Remember, the right side is the right side, providing you with a good view of the women with their swept-up hairdos.

In the far corner, back on the right side, sits Alice Mason, who sells billionaires apartments at prices starting at $3 million. She has clients who will pay anything to get the right flat in the right location. Alice entertains Nouvelle Society at home, but she is a Le Cirque regular at lunch. She earns those commissions, because no matter how much cash a client has, buying an apartment can pose sticky problems, depending on the board. Co-op boards do not like bachelors, for example, especially bachelor designers. And they definitely turn thumbs down on movie stars and entertainers. Most of them aren't keen on diplomats either, and they shy away from people who are in the gossip columns, who are divorced, or who are living together. They definitely don't like pets—especially big dogs.

One of the most formidable heads of any co-op board is Betty Sherrill, who heads the decorating firm of McMillen. Potential buyers into her Sutton Place South building are terrified to come in front of her. Casey Ribicoff, the wife of Abe Ribicoff, the former senator from Connecticut, consulted her friends before facing the formidable Mrs. Sherrill. Bill Blass, who is the confidant of many women on more than just their clothes, gave his best advice to Mrs. Ribicoff before she went before Mrs. Sherrill: "Just shut up, and wear a Waspy bow in your hair." The Ribicoffs got in, and now they have a lovely apartment overlooking the East River.

But today at Le Cirque, more is going on than the buying and selling of apartments. Ronald O. Perelman, chief executive officer of Revlon, is sitting as usual by the door at the far end of the room. Perelman, who is one of the richest men in America, rarely misses a trick, whether he is trying to buy Gillette, buy into Salomon Brothers, or just buy lunch. Every day when he arrives at Le Cirque, with a flick of the wrist he positions a small cushion at the back of his

chair. Sitting as always on the outside of the table, he
pleasure in greeting every passerby. With his wife, C
Cohen, the gossip columnist, he remains on the edge of
Nouvelle Society, taking in its seemingly endless comings
and goings.

Across the room, Saul Steinberg—short but impeccably
dressed in a dark suit—is celebrating his birthday with
members of his staff. Mostly in their thirties, they are also
in dark suits, and every one of them is smoking a cigar, like
all good baby tycoons are expected to do.

For months the Steinbergs had been planning daughter
Laura's wedding, and on April 18, 1988, it finally happened
—the most expensive party in New York history (nobody is
talking for the record, but the word is it cost $2 million
plus). "There's been nothing like it since a Vanderbilt married an Astor," marveled a member of the Old Guard. The
only inexpensive item for the evening was the rental of the
Metropolitan Museum. Because Steinberg's company is a
corporate sponsor, the Met received only $30,000 for the
event.

When Laura Steinberg walked into the Metropolitan Museum on the arm of her new husband, Jonathan Tisch, to
greet their five hundred guests, they entered a vast room
awash with twelve thousand white tulips (at $9.00 a tulip),
lilies everywhere, fifty thousand French roses (at $7.50 a
rose), and a forest of dogwood branches. The flower bill
alone, according to the New York Flower Market, was $1
million, to say nothing of the hand-painted marbleized
dance floor, complete with an inlaid gold wreath entwined
with the couple's initials, a trompe l'oeil wall, and other
walls draped with a cream muslin fabric. Each chair was
monogrammed, and trumpeters in medieval costumes
called the guests to a dinner of poached Coho salmon in a
pink champagne aspic, a trio of veal, lamb, and chicken
served with orzo, and porcini and spring vegetables.

The wines came from the Steinbergs' personal cellar: a

1982 Roederer Cristal (with a sprig of lily of the valley in each glass), a Corton Charlemagne Domaine Bonneau 1984, and a 1973 Château Latour.

The bride was radiant in antique white silk taffeta with a draped off-the-shoulder neckline and a seven-foot train embroidered with tiny sparkling stones in a Tudor floral design of white silk threads outlined in gold. Arnold Scaasi, the favorite designer of the Nouvelles, completed his masterpiece of a wedding dress with a tulle veil held in place by an antique diamond-and-pearl tiara.

Forget for a moment the time, expense, and effort that went into the biggest and grandest Nouvelle Society wedding to date. Was Laura a glorious bride and did everybody have a good time? Yes on both counts. The guest list mixed familiar names from the worlds of publishing, real estate, finance, and sports. Columnist Liz Smith filed an ecstatic report in the *Daily News,* and her friend archaeologist Iris Love caught the bridal bouquet. As the guests left the Great Hall, they had to wend their way through a crowd of carnival-dressed dancers rocking to the strains of a Brazilian orchestra. How I would have liked to be invited to that one! Much more interesting than the dreary Wasp festivities I usually attend.

The door of the restaurant opens again, and there stands Mrs. Alfred Taubman, blond tresses intact and figure perfect. After all, she is a former Miss Israel. Together with Carolyne Kravis, she is one of the leaders of Nouvelle Society and annually follows the élite to the Salzburg Music Festival, reserved, in days of yore, only for the exclusives: people like Oscar de la Renta, Lady Grace Dudley, and Count Brando Brandolini.

Taubman can be supersensitive to any suggestions that he and Judy engage in Nouvelle Society excesses. When *W* reported that Judy once sent the Taubman jet from New York to Palm Beach to pick up a pair of favorite shoes,

Alfred wrote me a witty, intelligent letter saying it just wasn't true. We offered to run a retraction but Taubman declined.

With Le Cirque filled to capacity most of the time, Sirio cannot help but feel proud when he thinks about the old days when he was headwaiter at the Colony, the home of what used to be called Café Society and was later the resting place for the Jet Set. Today he shepherds the Nouvelles, and he isn't above writing a concerned personal note when one of them stays away too long.

Photographers are banned inside Le Cirque, but Sirio is always happy to tell the press just who is inside. And always posted ouside, rain or shine, is the eager Bill Cunningham, long-time freelancer for *The New York Times.* Cunningham is always the one best informed about who is lunching with whom, because his number-one lady friend is the restaurant's official flower arranger. He regularly catches anyone of consequence as they enter or leave. Today former President Nixon fills his view-finder, together with a visiting Japanese businessman in traditional garb.

Inside, Barbara Walters is sharing a table with Mollie Parnis, and the talk is all of Carol and Punch Sulzberger's new London town house. According to Parnis, "Punch is just mad about houses." (Rather shy and only occasionally part of the Nouvelle scene, the Sulzbergers may have to change their lives now that he has become chairman of the board at the Met.) As we leave the restaurant, Barbara Walters is still conferring with Mollie Parnis. How these women love to talk.

I hope you're starting to understand why places like Le Cirque, La Grenouille, and La Côte Basque are so important to *W* and *WWD.* Except for a few private parties, where else can you see so many women looking their determined best, and where else can the Nouvelles trumpet their power and wealth so publicly?

Speaking of grand entrances, though, I cannot close without noting the effect of Jackie Kennedy Onassis's almost legendary appearances. It's hard to believe: at theaters, audiences stop talking; in restaurants, they stop eating. And when she goes to small charity events such as the Literary Lions dinners at the New York Public Library, even the most hardened members of society elbow their way toward her to get a closer look or, best of all, to be recognized. She is still the Celebrity of Celebrities.

At the Literary Lions affair in '86, I suddenly found myself face to face with her. Even though we had talked before and corresponded, in not-too-friendly terms, during her White House years, I could only mumble, "Hello, Jackie." She looked at me and responded, politely but coolly, "Good evening, Mr. Fairchild." Naturally, I regretted the whole night that I had called her "Jackie" and not "Mrs. Onassis." (Incidentally, Jackie—oops, Mrs. Onassis—has an unusual trick that I think must be hers alone. When she sees a photographer approaching, her eyes seem to open to their fullest aperture and glow into the lens, just as the strobe flash goes off.)

When it comes to dining or lunching out, Mrs. Onassis is rarely seen at the restaurants favored by Nouvelle Society. Buzzing around the city in her Big Apple taxi, she seems to do more shopping than eating. In any case, Le Cirque is definitely not her watering spot.

Not all of New York's lunch-outs want to be seen all of the time. Some of the biggest tycoons often prefer the Bar Room at The Four Seasons, precisely because they can achieve some privacy in that austere but spacious high-ceilinged chamber, somewhat reminiscent of the grand saloon in the old *Normandie.*

Architect Philip Johnson must like his own handiwork, because when he is in town he regularly lunches there, in the far booth. (There are only six booths, so every day there is a well-mannered scuffle to see who gets which.) Seating problems are resolved by a canny Swiss named Alex von Bidder.

Today two booths are occupied already, one by Mr. Johnson, who has just approved a new carpet for the room, the other by Henry Kissinger. Another booth is soon claimed by Si Newhouse, who, with his brother, Donald, sports the second-largest fortune in America: $7.5 billion flowing from an empire of newspapers, slick magazines, and cable television systems. The food arrives, and Newhouse tucks his napkin into his shirt collar. He is lunching today with Anna Wintour, newly named editor of *House & Garden.* In the summer of '88, she became editor of *Vogue,* and so up the Condé Nast ladder she climbs with those beautiful long legs.

Once ensconced in your booth in the Bar Room, you cannot be overheard except by the headwaiter, Julian, who not only tells his customers what they must eat and drink but sometimes tastes their food as well and drops a few gossipy tidbits of his own. Today Newhouse is cutting a deal, Ed Kosner is cooking up a hot story for *New York* Magazine, and Tina Brown, another Condé Nast star and the editor of *Vanity Fair,* will be along soon.

The men are just as sensitive as the women—maybe they're even more sensitive—about where they sit at lunch at The Four Seasons. I suppose it's a macho demonstration of power and influence, the male equivalent of the social minuet that takes place every day at Le Cirque. As the lunch hour ends, the sunlight filters through the chain curtain that cloaks the windows of the Bar Room. How sad a restaurant is without people—so impersonal—even though a few lonely types (are they out of work, or don't they have any other place to go?) begin to arrive at the bar and slip onto their stools.

Let us leave them perched there with their private thoughts and briefly list a few of *W*'s recent Ins and Outs before we go back to the office.

1. Mrs. Vincent (Brooke) Astor: The Queen of New York keeps the city's institutions alive and perking, not just through Astor Foundation contributions ($160 million at last count) but because she works night and day. As we have already seen, she was the first to accept Nouvelle Society, warts and all. You guessed it: In with a big *I*.
2. In places to give: The New York Public Library; the Metropolitan Museum.
3. Annette Reed: her brains and stamina work magic on the powerful men of New York. One of the princesses of New York, she, together with Mrs. Astor, keeps the library and the Met alive and well. In.
4. Pat Buckley, wife of William F. Buckley, commentator, author, and editor. He has the title, but she is the organizer of many events that are good for New York. Shares Princess of the City honors with Annette Reed. In.
5. John Gutfreund: He's In, but his good-looking wife, Susan (the Mother of Nouvelle Society), is Out, because she is silly.
6. Mrs. Jayne Wrightsman: Grandly In with a few.
7. Henry Kravis: A gentleman of Nouvelle Society, he is In, in spite of the fact that he is the King of the Leveraged Buyouts. His wife, designer Carolyne Roehm, is also In, even though she changes her contact lenses from blue to green to blue.
8. James Wolfensohn: The big-money banker from Australia, who almost single-handedly rebuilt beautiful Carnegie Hall, is In.
9. Felix Rohatyn: The Lazard Frères banker, who merges and buys and then sells American companies to foreigners but then turns around and criticizes the practice in *The New York Review of Books,* is Out.
10. Arthur (Punch) Sulzberger: The board chairman of the Metropolitan Museum is In. He's not been a big con-

tributor to the Met, but he brings the power of *The New York Times.* To be In, you don't join clubs anymore, just the board of the Met or the library. Membership fees begin at $1 million and go on up, depending on who you are.

11. Author John Richardson, Met executive vice-president Ashton Hawkins, and Charles Ryskamp, director of the Frick Museum: These three In Walkers influence Astor and Reed.

12. Jerry Zipkin: Out, even before Nancy left the White House.

13. Saul and Gayfryd Steinberg: He's another buyout trader. They're the most Out couple of Nouvelle Society. Talk about conspicuous, frightening spending!

14. Donald Trump: The real-estate mogul, who is best at promoting himself, is Out, but Ivana, his wife, who speaks frankly about everything, including herself, is In.

15. Restaurants: La Grenouille—In, because of the lighting at night, the private upstairs dining room with fireplace, and, often, the food. Le Cirque—Out: too full of Nouvelle Society and dyed golden "Cirque hair" à la the two Palms, Beach and Springs (also Out). The Four Seasons—Out for food, In for show-off power.

16. More Out people: Nan Kempner and Anne Bass (too aggressive) and Mercedes Bass and Mica Ertegun (the queens of savage social climbing).

17. The Rockefellers and the Dillons: In, but Out of the Savage Set, replaced by the Nouvelles—Kravis, Gutfreund, the Tisches, et al.

18. The John Kluges: Though among America's richest ($3.2 billion), they are Out, in spite of being friends with Prince Charles. Historically, British royalty associate with the very rich. A good Englishman never likes to spend his own money; the Brits invented the verb "to sponge."

19. Out: Most movie and television stars, directors, and producers. California tackiness is their domain.
20. In: English theater and movie stars.
21. Out: Television commentators and politicians.
22. In: New York. (Fifth Avenue is the only place to live; the West Side is still Out.)
23. Out: The press breaking into Nouvelle Society. The only reporters who belong there are Suzy, Miss Scoop of the New York *Post,* and Liz Smith, Miss Cause Célèbre of the *Daily News.* If you play the game Snakes and Ladders, they are must reading and constitute Home. Barbara Walters is Out.
24. Out: International news; but national news (exception: politics) and local news are In.
25. In: Pamela Harriman, but she's out of power. She just can't make a President anymore.
26. Out: John Fairchild, who conceived the original In and Out list, and this one as well.

Finally, always remember that anyone who's Out today could be In next time. It's that kind of world.

THE GREATEST
OF THEM ALL

We dressed Jackie O. in Gaultier. She looks great even in this rubberized tank dress (1).

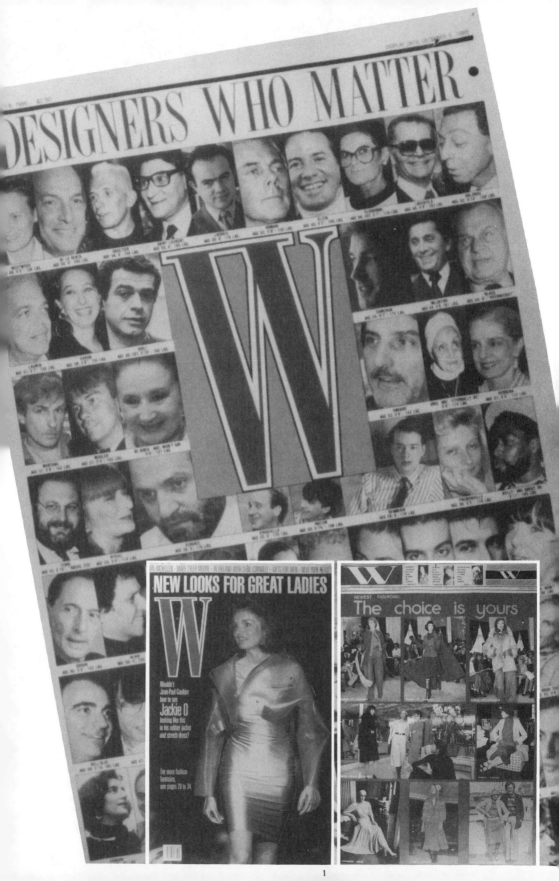

DESIGNERS WHO MATTER

NEW LOOKS FOR GREAT LADIES

Wouldn't
Jean-Paul Gaultier
love to see
Jackie O
looking like this
in his rubber jacket
and stretch dress?

For more fashion
fantasies,
see pages 29 to 34.

The choice is yours

1

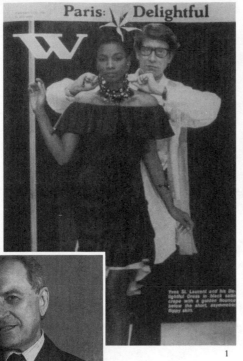

Y ves Saint Laurent, King of fashion, endures as Coco Chanel (1). His business partner, Pierre Bergé, is head of the Paris Opera (2). Both YSL and Bergé are "divas."

1

2

3

4

Saint Laurent in a happier moment with his muses LouLou Klossowski and blond Veronica Lake-style Betty Catroux (3).

YSL covered in lilies after another triumph (4).

1

2

3

W *Original Beauties*

La Belle Helene

The Italian Way — Pages 83 to 96   The Sensuous Furs — Pages 98 to 127

YSL with fashion priestess Diana Vreeland (1); with movie star Catherine Deneuve wearing, *of course*, YSL (2).
Cover girl Hélène Rochas—Paris's Queen of Beauty (3). Nothing to do with Rochas perfume anymore.

Ann Getty with one of America's top designers, Donna Karan (4). Betsy Bloomingdale, Jacques Chazot, and Nan Kempner (5). John Fairchild with Christa Worthington and Françoise Fabius, wife of the former French Prime Minister (6).

YSL living in Marrakech style (1). YSL in his Proustian dream Château Gabriel, Normandy (2).

Christian Lacroix, the master of fantasy fashion and personal charm (3).

3

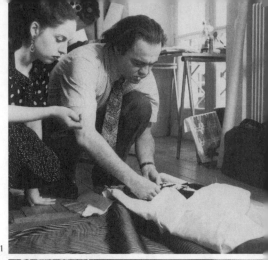

Lacroix at work, with his magic touch. Sometimes his clothes seem removed from reality but are always dreamily romantic (1, 2).

1

2

Karl Lagerfeld sitting at the foot of his Marie Antoinette bed (3). Intelligent, witty, rattling on like a machine gun, he has lots to say about everything and everyone.
Cover boy Lagerfeld with his once favorite model Inès (4), who is now the model for "La Marianne de France,"
His own collection, not for Chanel (5).

3

4

5

Ungaro stands in front of his 13th-century home, La Cavalerie, in Provence (1). He's as strong as the stones of the region. His clothes are femme fatale to the end.

1

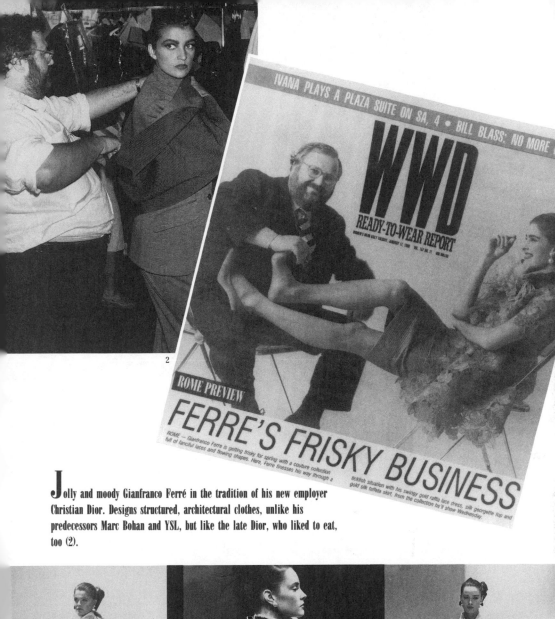

ROME PREVIEW

FERRE'S FRISKY BUSINESS

ROME — Gianfranco Ferré is getting frisky for spring with a couture collection full of fanciful laces and flowing shapes. Here, Ferre finesses his way through a ticklish situation with his swingy gold raffia lace dress, silk georgette top and gold silk taffeta skirt, from the collection he'll show Wednesday.

J olly and moody Gianfranco Ferré in the tradition of his new employer Christian Dior. Designs structured, architectural clothes, unlike his predecessors Marc Bohan and YSL, but like the late Dior, who liked to eat, too (2).

V alentino, the Sheik of Chic, designs rich froufrou, your-money's-worth clothes. Cover boy Valentino poses in costume with court (1).

1

The Chic with his shrewd business partner Giancarlo Giammetti. Their living style resembles their clothes (2).

2

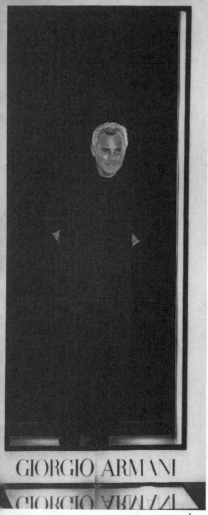

GIORGIO ARMANI

1

Italian Chic

Giorgio Armani is Modern Italian Chic—
minimal in look, maximum in quality.

2

Giorgio Armani, the Jesuit monk of fashion—pure, elegant, modern, and always influential (1). He is copied by the fashion world.
Donna Karan. A determined designer and woman (2). Her style very in the Armani mode, but more feminine.

Gianni Versace, the Barnum of Italian fashion—enough to say "very Versace" (1).
Vivienne Westwood, English eccentric all the way. That's why the male designers adore her fashions and of course copy them (2).

Bill Blass at home in New Preston, Connecticut. George Washington stopped there too (3).
First Lady Barbara Bush at a press conference was asked by WWD reporter Susan Watters if she found living in the White House romantic. Her answer: "What a ridiculous question." (4).
Mariuccia Mandelli blitzkrieged her Krizian knits into a great fortune (5).
Mary McFadden—her fine American Wasp family didn't stop her from designing sometimes odd, sometimes beautiful, fashions, as exotic as she is in her life (6).

Ralph Lauren has designed his version of the Wobbly Wasps into a $2.8 billion yearly business. His 72nd Street store is an ode to Lauren and makes for the smartest shopping in the world (1).

Looking like a cowboy, Lauren, chaps and all, "ranches out" in Colorado before jumping into his Waspy jalopy for a ride downtown (2).

3

6

Pierre Cardin says he is one of the richest men in France (10th)—his name licensed on everything from soup to nuts—and he owns some of the choicest real estate in many countries (3).

Calvin Klein, another billionaire stylist/merchandiser, cuddles with his wife, Kelly (4).

On the cover of *W* he runs through the fields with his models (5).

His partner, Barry Schwartz, with his wife, Sheryl (6), loves race horses, stamps and investment, and takes loving care of his childhood pal—Calvin.

5

4

Calvin Klein Jeans

Enough to say Calvin Klein.

Calvin Klein Jeans

Calvin Klein Underwear

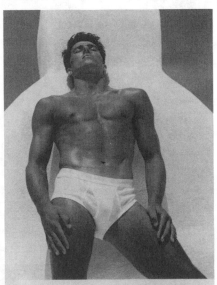

Calvin Klein Underwear

He has built his empire and name on advertisements that whet the sexual appetite he himself understands so well. *Calvin Klein advertisements © CRK Advertising; photographs Bruce Webber.*

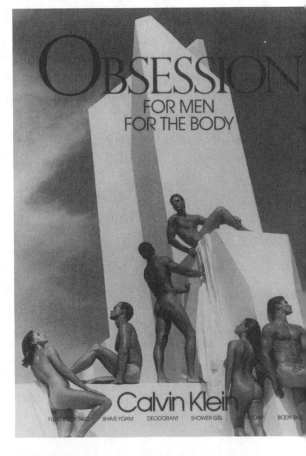

OBSESSION
FOR MEN
FOR THE BODY

Calvin Klein

Coco Chanel at eighty-two still waving, working night and day, reigned as the empress of all fashion. Years after her death, her fashion party is never over, and she must be laughing at all the male designers who can't even touch her (1). Gustav Zumsteg, the King of Fabrics. Swiss art collector, restaurateur, he gives his best cuts to YSL (2).

1

2

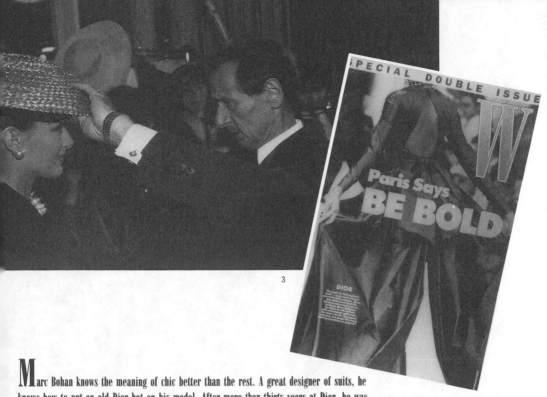

3

Marc Bohan knows the meaning of chic better than the rest. A great designer of suits, he knows how to put an old Dior hat on his model. After more than thirty years at Dior, he was retired with more than $2 million, but he will return (3).

Hubert de Givenchy—"Le Grand"—lives in elegant, grand style. His taste for houses (he has four), and all the trappings, is the best in the fashion group (4).

4

Arnold Scaasi (1). The Wasps love his frothy fashion and so does First Lady Barbara Bush. Claude Montana, the Robert Redford of France. He is a master of tailoring and of runway showmanship (2).

1

3

4

Geoffrey Beene (3). "Above fashion," says the *New York Times* (whatever that means). Doesn't speak to *WWD* or *W*. I have never met Samuel Albert Bozeman, Jr. (his real name).

Roy "Halston" Froick carried American sportswear into the couture, making sportswear snobbish and elegant (4). Victor Costa carries "fashion secrets" in his briefcase. He is the best copyist and sometimes makes a couture original more wearable (5).

1

2

3

4

<big>O</big>scar de la Renta, Europeanized with exotic Latin touches, fits his model (1).

At home with his late wife, Françoise, the first real general of Nouvelle Society (2).

With his models (3).

The Latin lover de la Renta is always on the move. In Italy (4, center), with (R–L) the sheik Valentino, Nancy Kissinger, Giancarlo Giammetti, and Valentino's PR girl Georgina Brandolini.

5

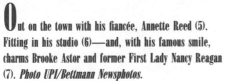
Out on the town with his fiancée, Annette Reed (5). Fitting in his studio (6)—and, with his famous smile, charms Brooke Astor and former First Lady Nancy Reagan (7). *Photo UPI/Bettmann Newsphotos.*

6

7

The ultimate Fashion Victims in the
same Bill Blass dress: Judy Peabody,
fighter for AIDS sufferers (1, left); and
pistol-packing Texan Lynn Wyatt. André
Oliver, one of Paris's most elegant
gentlemen, is in the middle.
James Galanos, California's best designer,
copes with Beverly Morsey and Lillian
Fluor wearing his same dress (2).

8

WOBBLY WASPS

One of our best-selling cover ideas for *W* and one of our most talked-about issues was inspired by—and thank goodness for them—the Georgica Association. We will always be grateful.

The association, which takes pride in its historical longevity, is a private compound of summer residences in which Wobbly Wasps reside, far from New York's Nouvelle Society, in Wainscott, Long Island. Though Wainscott is between Bridgehampton and East Hampton, these Wobblies don't mix with any of the

Hamptons. Nor, for that matter, do they commingle with the rest of Long Island or New York.

I can speak with some authority about the Georgica Association because Jill and I became members of this enclave and spent too much—Wasps like me don't like to spend money—trying to restore a ramshackle, badly designed cottage into its cute Waspy state. The association's Wobbly Wasps live in tumbledown cottages, some small, some large.

In front of our gray clapboard structure with its Canadian cedar-shingled roof (Wasp musts: clapboard and cedar shingles) stood several huge pine trees, all slightly wobbly. We decided they would have to come down so they wouldn't fall into our bedroom. I was staring at the pines, thinking we really couldn't bear to destroy a tree, when a yellow Datsun pulled up. It had a dented fender and mud all over it (a Wasp must: never a big or shiny car). The car was muddy because the Georgica Association, sticklers for tradition, maintained dirt roads (a Wasp must-not: macadam). Out of the Datsun popped a tiny lady, as thin as Olive Oyl. "Mr. Fairchild," she said, "I am Polly Livingston. Livingston, as in George Washington-Livingston." It took several moments before I realized that Mrs. Livingston was letting me know she was somehow related to our first President, father of the real Wasps. She quickly got to the point: "We don't approve of you taking down those pines," she told me in a soft but biting accent. Then, jumping back into her car, she zoomed off in a cloud of dust. Her car was barely out of sight when click inside my head came the Wobbly Wasp cover.

When Jill and I went to bed that night above the garage (Wasps love garage apartments) we heard strange voices from outside. Our next-door neighbors, the Hayeses, were in our garden. And what they were saying about our reconstruction of the cottage and the redoing of our garden didn't exactly lull us to sleep.

"Why didn't they leave well enough alone?" asked Mrs. Hayes. "Look at that picture window. My God, Al, just look at it." Wasps would rather go without a view and even without light than have a picture window.

The next morning we looked at the window and were convinced they were right about it. We consoled ourselves that our window was at least semi-Wasp, given the individual panes. Anyway, it was too late to change anything.

The following night, someone climbed up to the roof of our garage, right above our heads, and stole our weather vane, a lovely horse (Wasps love weather vanes by the sea).

And then the next morning I saw Mrs. Hayes hanging her wash next to our privet hedge. The wash flapped away in the sea breeze as we sat under an old apple tree, having lunch outside our new Georgica cottage for the first time. Looking at the wash was too much: we might as well have been in Newark. Flap, flap, flap went the polyester-cotton sheets (Wasps think polyester is practical), making us think we were at sea on a two-masted schooner. Would the privet grow high enough so we wouldn't see the wash? Should we take the privet out and plant a jungle? But the privet had just been replanted and moved away from the Hayeses' property line because they had complained that it was hanging over their land. (Yes, Wasps are very concerned with their property lines. So are the French. They won't even let a neighbor's branch extend onto their land.)

Wasps are greatly concerned about boundaries and borders, and where other people can and cannot go. During the season, a permanent guard stands at the gate to the Georgica Association, protecting the compound from outsiders, even from those who want only to pass through on their way to the beach. And those who *rent* inside the Georgica Association are not permitted to amble down the dirt road to the beach. They must go around to Beach Lane and approach the beach through the town road.

What do you do, therefore, when you have a friend like author Irwin Shaw, who rents the Murphy House on the pond (Wasps love to rent their rundown houses with worn chintz for big prices) and who's coming to see you for lunch? Yes, he can walk from his house down the dirt road to ours, but if we want to take a swim before lunch, he doesn't have the right to continue down the private road to the beach house, and furthermore he's not allowed on the beach because he's not a member.

So we jumped into the car and left the Georgica Association, went down Beach Lane to the town beach, walked from it to the cordoned-off Georgica Association beach, where the members of the association sat with their lunch-box sandwiches and pink gin. (Wasps love to picnic on the beach. They thought it very odd that we picnicked in our garden under the apple tree and drank a dry white burgundy.) Down the beach we went, as eyes swiveled in our direction. Were they worried we would stop and sit with them? They knew better. On we went, past the women of Georgica, in their flower-printed bathing suits with demure little skirts, leftovers from their grandmothers' day. Modest and prim Waspy women sitting in a row on the beach pecking like chickens at everyone around them.

After our walk, we had dinner together, and Irwin, who rarely set foot in the kitchen, prepared his own version of broiled bluefish. (I always called it glue fish. I don't eat blues unless I have to.) His recipe: broil the blues with mayonnaise. And even I ate it, while Irwin, as usual, entertained us. He looked like a big grizzly bear but acted more like a lovable teddy.

At times, association members asked why we didn't sit on the beach instead of going for long walks. (Wasps like to sit and stare, but they're not much for walking long distances. They prefer burning to a crisp in the sun to get that Waspy, weathered look, so often abetted by drink.)

The one day Jill and I did stop and sit, decorators Vincent Fourcade and Bob Denning came strolling down the public beach toward us. I saw them approaching in their very French bikinis (a Wasp never wears a bikini) and as they got closer, we waved. I got up to greet them, and the members stopped talking, stopped eating, stopped drinking, and turned their eyes on the bikini intruders. We were happy to see them, our friends.

After Fourcade and Denning left, Beba Hayes, the Queen of Georgica Waspdom, asked us, "Who were those fellows?" I explained that they were important New York decorators who lived in that wonderful Gimbel house with the blue shutters on Beach Lane in back of the Georgica Association. Members of the association did not approve of Beach Lane because several Europeans including the offspring of Suni Agnelli had moved there and gave, "they had heard," wild parties.

Mrs. Hayes listened to me skeptically while I tried to impress her with our friends and interrupted to say: "Never heard of them. And who ever uses a decorator anyway?"

She wouldn't have been happy to know that Denning and Fourcade had been urging us to "de-Wasp" our cottage. They had brought us little weeping beech trees (a non-Waspy plant) for our garden. And Denning, looking at our plasterboard ceiling (Wasps think real plaster is too expensive for a summer cottage), had suggested we put floral wallpaper between the old beams.

That summer in the Hamptons, we had few visitors for two reasons. For one thing, it was difficult to entertain. Our kitchen was too small and the Garland range (Wasps love six-burner gas stoves) was too big. It was hard to get into the kitchen, which was separated from the living room by only half a wall and a small door. One day, though, we invited Estée Lauder for luncheon. She arrived wearing a very impressive veiled Givenchy hat. It had been worn at Le Cirque, but never in Wainscott. In the world of the Georgica Association, hats were worn only to shield one from the sun.

The second reason we didn't entertain was that when we took our guests into the garden all the Georgicans kept riding by on their bicycles to stare through our privet hedge (Wasps are into English bicycles, which they leave out in the rain so they look used). When, for example, Lee Radziwill and her ex-sister-in-law Pat Kennedy Lawford came to luncheon, even Paul, the policeman who patrolled the area, knew they had been there. (Wasps always know what other Wasps are up to. Paul informed us one day that a member of the association had chased his wife out of their house with a Revolutionary War rifle. The wife had hidden under a bush until Paul rescued her.)

The reason I have gone into all these details about Wobbly Wasps is quite simple. They are an endangered species. Their ranks are thinning out. Partly because if Waspdom is not in your blood, trying to live a Wasp existence in Georgica usually doesn't work.

Before Donald Trump became a real-estate and media star, he and Ivana rented a small cottage in the association behind a big sand dune, a stone's throw from the beach. They were between the town beach and the private Georgica beach, so they had no problem getting to the sand. But given the humble cottage and the Waspy association, it wasn't long before they packed up and trundled off to Trump Tower, to Palm Beach, and to purchase yachts.

One day, designer Ralph Lauren, who has done a great job of turning the world into pseudo-Wasps, paid us a visit. But when this admirer of Waspdom pulled into our driveway in his open Jeep and took off his Lauren dark glasses (resembling Porsche glasses), I'm sure he was not impressed by what he saw. He found our house, as he admitted, small and too close to the neighbors. He was disillusioned. He thought that Long Island Wasps summering in Georgica lived in a much grander style.

When Ralph came into our house with his wife, Ricky, she, too, wondered how all of us could fit into this little cottage. They asked why we had constructed a "stalag"-type chain-link fence separating our property from the Whitneys' (this Whitney was no relation to the Long Island North Shore Jock Whitneys, royals among the Wasps). We explained that it wasn't our fence. We had tried to cover it with rose bushes, but they never grew because every fall the Whitneys' pool was emptied onto our property, flooding out the roses. The Laurens drove us over to their house behind the dunes on the sea. They had rented a large Cape Cod cottage that had been transported, piece by piece, from Massachusetts. It was owned by a rich Wasp family. Ricky, with the help of her cook, had baked raisin cookies, and we sat down to coffee and cookies. In a real Waspy household, it would have been tea.

Wasps cannot hold back the tide of materialism, especially when it comes to cars: BMWs and Mercedes station wagons. I remember a family in New Canaan, Connecticut—which vies with Greenwich for the title of richest city-town in America—in which each of the four children had his or her own car, as did the husband and wife. Fortunately, their stately stone house, with its three-story white columns (Wasps like columns) had a long driveway with a big parking area.

New Canaan is a town with a common (Wasps love to think they are New England born and bred, even if they aren't). New Canaan is also a town where life is built around "the club" (with long waiting lists; Wasps often must join second-rate and even third-rate clubs). At Friday-night buffets and Saturday-night dances, the Wasps of New Canaan gather together in tribal rituals for which the women are carefully dressed (never flashily—that's for New York) with little white pearls on their swanlike necks. Waspy women don't seem to age: they just weather from the sun, sea, and drink.

But when Wasp tycoons began traveling all over the world with their wives, corruption à la Nouvelle Society began creeping in. Waspy wives no longer wanted to stay at home, running houses with inadequate, highly paid sub-urban maids. The women of New Canaan, therefore, hired cleaning services to invade their big houses: burly men spring-cleaned from attic to basement in one big sweep. Dinner parties became rare, but catered cocktail parties that went on for hours flourished.

And the New Canaan housewife had freed herself to cir-cle the globe in royal style with her tycoon husband. Imag-ine the head of a large oil company meeting Ari Onassis and several Arab oil sheiks on his yacht. Imagine the talk when Mrs. New Canaan returned home bearing gifts (sometimes jewels) from these potentates. By comparison, the quiet, pastoral life of New Canaan was Dullsville.

So the Wasps flew back to apartments in the very Man-hattan they had wanted to escape because it was filled with "the wrong people." And they started making the scene. Lunch and dinner at the Colony Club (for women), Links and Brook (for men), and the River Club (for both sexes). Now the "exclusive" clubs where Wasps nested only with other Wasps and dined on chicken salad and buffet food were not enough. French and Italian restaurants lured Wasps from as far away as Texas. They escaped from their stately homes and began entertaining in style. Their lives were changing.

Wasps from out of town become more aggressive than

New Yorkers when they get to the city. It must be something in the Manhattan air. I know this all too well from close personal experience. A group of us had given the first fund-raising party for the School of American Ballet. When Sid and Anne Bass invaded New York from Fort Worth, Anne Bass joined the committee, and in a matter of weeks she had taken over. The rest of us resigned. She wrote each of us a strong letter, asking "how dare" (her words) we do that.

Then, quite suddenly, as we know, Sid Bass ran away from Anne Bass (who stayed with her love, the New York City Ballet) to take up with Mercedes Kellogg, who was married at the time to Ambassador Francis Kellogg, a fine Wasp in the truest sense. Mercedes rocked the city, putting a smile on everyone's face. At private parties at Mortimer's, a restaurant that has become almost a club for Wasps, Mercedes danced on a table, while a smitten Sid Bass sat by and watched, enjoying every moment. Sid and Mercedes moved into the Hotel Carlyle, where Wasps and others rest their weary heads between marriages. They were at every party as the New Couple of the Moment. Mercedes and Sid stayed out late at parties, returning to the Carlyle, where they requested Waspy tunes like "Begin the Beguine" or danced in their $1,000-a-day suite until the wee hours of the morning.

Meanwhile, Anne Bass was Concording to Europe for fittings and for meals in all the best restaurants.

Wasp love stories can be frightfully intense. The head of a television network was sitting next to a princess of New York society at dinner one night, when he announced that his marriage was all over. He was filing for divorce and would never return to that boring life in New Canaan. No more TV every Friday night for him. He was smitten with the New York life and had decided to enjoy all the parties. He was now a Wasp in a powerful position, with strings attached to the wild world of show business, not the snoozing suburbs. After his pronouncement, he jokingly said to his dinner princess, "Let's run off together."

We Wasps can say what we want about the Nouvelles and their ways, even ridicule them behind their backs, but secretly we are jealous (a real Waspy trait). We don't want to be them—no way—but we can't help accepting their wonderful invitations. They do entertain better—not just more lavishly—and they do exude warmth. Try an all-Wasp evening. They've all been to school together, they've all vacationed together at Hobe Sound, they all want their children to marry other Wasps with more money. Wasps rewrap old Christmas gifts and give them to friends. Waspy women, no matter how rich they are, always try to buy their clothes on sale, though their husbands are crazy about all sorts of machines and gadgets (especially underground sprinkling systems, which remind them of the golf course). Wasps are driven around town or to the airport by the local policeman, never by a chauffeur, preferably in a $35,000 Mercedes diesel station wagon, and they're always concerned about their financial situation even though they are rich enough. And whether they work or not, they're concerned about how hard they work.

My favorite Wasp story is about me. When one Wasp plays a trick on another Wasp, watch out. One of my best friends is a lawyer who wears copies of Brooks Brothers suits made to order in Hong Kong and rubbers to restaurants at even a hint of rain or snow. We'd lunched together often over the past twenty years, and he had never paid. Finally, I told him outright that it was time he did. He agreed. On the appointed day, I arrived early at La Côte Basque. In he came, clutching a small box he deposited in the checkroom. (I decided he'd left his rubbers at home and had to buy a new pair.) He approached the table, and even before he sat down, announced that he had no money with him because he'd just spent it on a new pair of shoes.

"Don't worry," I told him. "I opened a charge account here in your name."

He was speechless until it was time to order the wine, and then he let out a Waspy snort and said, "You mean I have to pay for the wine too?"

But I have another story for you. When Jill and I were informed by Edward Lee Cave, New York's top real-estate agent, that he might have a buyer for our large apartment at 10 Gracie Square, in true Waspy fashion I complained that the offer wasn't high enough.

"After all," I said, "our apartment is in impeccable condition [we hadn't redecorated in twenty years], we have the best kitchen in New York, and a fabulous view."

Cave paused before responding, then said, "You might think so, but the prospective buyer finds the bathroom with the iron coming through the porcelain in the bathtubs antiquated, the air-conditioning needs updating, and so does the kitchen. John, the apartment is just a little tired and needs lots of work and lots of money." I was furious. Boiling. Just like a typical Wobbly Wasp. No doubt about it. We Wasps are an endangered species.

Still, there are the real Wasps, I mean Waspdom's élite. Those Invisible People who, unlike pseudos like me (I am proud to say I have Irish blood from my Grandmother Boyd), come from pure or impure English Stock, are New England originally, and might have migrated to the West. They live among themselves, often in an elegant, quiet style. Let's look at a few of them:

Louis Auchincloss, novelist and King of the Wasps. Another Auchincloss, Douglas, a relative who walked more on the wild side, once told me that his side of the family were direct Scottish descendants of valets.

Paul Mellon, philanthropist, art collector, civilized man

of great taste, and the most respected of the Wasps. Banking is really a small part of his life. He has put his wealth to great use—and without fanfare—with donations of art to the National Gallery in Washington and to the museum he built at Yale University for English paintings he donated.

Warren Buffett, America's most brilliant investor, who thrills to making money but not having it and who has publicly stated he will leave his entire fortune to charity.

Thomas Watson, ex-chairman of IBM, who rocked Wasp society when he sent out telegrams to his friends announcing he and his wife, Olive, were separating, and then three weeks later sent out another telegram saying they were back together—happily.

The Whitney Wasps are divided into two camps: the Jock Whitneys of the North Shore of Long Island, where Jock's widow, Betsy, reigns quietly in the background as Queen of the Wasps. She goes out only to small intimate parties, and because of her frail health has a nurse always at her side. Nevertheless, she was seen at an AIDS benefit at Mortimer's. Betsy Whitney (daughter of the Boston brain surgeon Harvey Cushing) is considered "top drawer," to use a vulgar Wasp expression, for her fine taste. Her sister, Babe Paley, was one of the world's most elegant women and reigned as Queen of New York until her death in the '70s.

And then there are the other Whitneys: the C. V. Whitneys, commonly known as Sonny and Mary Lou. Mary Lou loves publicity, has a publicity agent, loves parties, rides through Saratoga, New York, like Scarlett O'Hara with her parasol open in a horse-drawn carriage. Sonny and Mary Lou give costume balls during the racing season. Most Wasps are mad for their dogs but Mary Lou went too far when at the owner-dog look-alike contest at the Saratoga Race Course she donned a tutu to look like her poodle Edelweiss. She won the "best tutu look-alike in the senior citizens' class."

Another Queen Wasp, Alice Tully (Miss; she never married but once was in love with an opera star), has kept New York in fine music with her generous gifts.

A matriarch of Waspdom is one of America's top decorators—May Parrish (a Boston Kinnicut). Better known as Sister, she decorated the homes of the rich, great Wasps but has shied away personally from giving her English–John Fowler—taste to Nouvelle Society.

Ninety-plus-year-old Sonny has made a great deal of money investing: he was one of the original investors in the movie *Gone With the Wind.*

After the Saratoga social season, the Whitneys move to their private 55,000-acre Adirondacks camp, Deerlands, on Tupper Lake. To ensure absolute privacy from the rest of the Whitney clan, Sonny and Mary Lou have strung a net across the lake so no canoes can get through to spy on their house.

Mary Lou is a practical woman, and when she saw the deer eating up the flowers in her window boxes, she planted artificial flowers. But no one is allowed to shoot Mary Lou's favorite deer, which are identified with white markings painted on their backsides. The other Whitneys refer to the C. V. Whitneys as "the fallen ones," because of their endless parties and personal P.R.

Defending like Jeanne D'Arc the Wasp tradition and the real Wasps is the formidable Permelia Ruby Reed, who rules over the Wasp presence in the sun—Hobe Sound, Florida. As long as eighty-plus-year-old Mrs. Reed is around, Hobe Sound is safe and secure from all foreign invaders—meaning almost everyone who is not Wasp or the right Wasp. Not that Permelia Reed doesn't stray from the Wasp fold. She campaigned for Dukakis in spite of the fact that her best friend is Dorothy Bush, President Bush's mother.

It was a most profitable deal when Mr. Reed (now deceased) purchased Hobe Sound and sold off the swampy land in lots to fellow Wasps. Wasps strike a hard deal with everyone and even harder with fellow Wasps. No one wants to be stung by a Wasp.

9
THE HIGH COURT OF FASHION

For the couture collections of fall and winter 1988 we made it to Paris without my misplacing my passport. On a previous trip I had traveled all the way to New York on the Concorde, that needlenose marvel of flight, without it. How? As a person momentarily without a country.

I had arrived at Charles de Gaulle Airport from the South of France with Roderick, my King Charles spaniel, and we had our boarding pass and seat number. As we went through Paris passport control, Roderick wagging his tail contentedly because he loved to people-watch at airports, I reached into my pocket for my billfold and found it but no passport. I was sure the passport was in the jacket which at that moment was being loaded onto the Concorde. The Air France woman was very sympathetic. She talked excitedly into a telephone, and my luggage was brought up in minutes. I quickly unpacked it and went through every pocket: no passport. Roderick looked as though he knew it all along. Then I remembered. My passport was in a sports jacket—a gray-and-white tweed Armani—hanging in my closet at Mas Daumas. But I had to get on that plane. I closed up the bag and went to the counter, desperate, and begged Air France to call the American Embassy. They did and then turned the telephone over to me. A friendly American voice asked: "How old are you? Where were you born? What do you do?" Then he spoke to Air France and again to me: "If the French let you on the plane, we will notify Kennedy to let you go back home." Before I could thank him, the voice noted with some pleasure, "Of course you are going to have to pay a fine at the other end. They will bill you." And the U.S. Government did: twenty-five dollars, and it was worth every penny.

Roderick and I were the last to board the Concorde, and we took our seat next to a distinguished-looking man who, I could see right away, was not *sympathique;* he did not like dogs or at least a dog sitting next to him on the Concorde. We didn't say a word. But I just had to go to the bathroom. I spoke to Roderick. "Stay there, please, Roderick, I will be right back." My dog seemed to understand. I had just closed the door to the toilet when suddenly the plane gave a lurch and turned to the right. I rushed out and there was Roderick sitting in the man's lap—both dog and man terrified. That broke the ice. The man and I talked and drank our red Bordeaux with pleasure all the way to New York.

By the way, I left my passport behind at the Ritz in Paris

only three days before writing these lines. But that time I wasn't so lucky. There was no way the French would let me leave and no way the Swiss would let me enter their well-guarded borders.

Now I am at the Ritz, my passport safely secured, and the collections so important to *WWD/W* are about to begin. My rooms overlooking the Place Vendôme are called the Coco Chanel suite, but I bet she never slept there. I can remember from my old days in Paris walking her back to the rue Cambon side of the Ritz and up to her small suite, which was nothing like the one I am in now. There were straps crisscrossing her bed. She told me that she had "violent" nightmares and had to be tied into her bed every night. I recently learned that those nightmares were brought on by morphine.

The Ritz has long been one of the world's greatest hotels. Everyone is catered to. Even a dog is given a special dark brown blanket, embossed with the words "Ritzy Dog," but Roderick still preferred the bed.

Now that the Ritz has been purchased by Egyptian tycoon Mohammed al-Fayed, who has invested some $350 million in it, it has become the most luxurious hotel in the world for the Nouvelle business man and woman. Underground is an incredible sports complex with terrycloth covering every machine in the gymnasium, an Olympic-size swimming pool (which can be covered over for a ball or even for a fashion show), and a grand Roman décor straight out of Caligula. On my tour of this monument to the vanity of the human body, I see many space-age machines enclosed in glass rooms. I ask what they are for. "For cellulite. You know, it removes unwanted fat." I point to another machine. "Oh, that scrapes away the face wrinkles, and over there are salt-water baths with seaweed to invigorate the tired body." I wear thick paper slippers over my shoes "to keep out the germs," but the guide wears spike high heels which, she insists, never go out onto the streets of Paris. I never do get around to working out in the Ritz sports club.

But my colleagues and I are right there front row center Sunday afternoon at the Hotel Intercontinental to see Christian Lacroix's first show after the pouf. We were invited in a warm personal letter to see Lacroix the day before as he put the finishing touches on his collection. We decided to wait to see what the most talked-about designer would do in the actual show. In previews there were simple clothes, straight and soft, a big change from the overworked and overworn pouf.

Now the collection starts out quietly, and ends on the same quiet note. There is some enthusiasm but the applause is reserved. The room is not buzzing. Before we have time to think about what we will write, NBC puts a microphone and bright lights right on us, a reporter pulls out her notes, and says she has questions Christy Ferer, her New York editor, wants answered "on camera." People are pushing and shoving to get out of the room while she begins rather aggressively, "Well, what do you think? Was it great? Was it as good as last time? You people helped make this man, now what do you think?"

And I say what I think is true: "Lacroix has a lot of guts to go against the fashion stream and make what he likes. Yes, he has guts." And that is all I will say. But I knew, because I had no tingles in my toes, that it was not a great show.

Despite the fact that Lacroix did not have a great collection, he still is one of the most important designers on the fashion scene, and thank God we have him around to write about, because there are slim pickings these days. We need to rise to the defense of an endangered species—great fashion designers.

It is only Sunday and we have only begun to see the shows. Lacroix may look better when stacked up against the other big guns: Saint Laurent, Ungaro, Lagerfeld for Chanel, and, to a lesser degree, Bohan, then at Dior, and Givenchy. After all, no one can rank the collections without first seeing all of them, noting all the trends, and putting designers and their ideas together.

Many times at the end of the season we have given star ratings to the Paris collections—one to four stars. And such ranking has led to unhappiness all around. So we have decided to leave the stars in the sky where they belong.

At the Ungaro show in the Musée des Arts Décoratifs panic sets in because the security is so tight. And to make matters worse the Ungaro guards spot outside the door the best copyist in the world: Victor Costa, Texas manufacturer, who has copied from all the top Paris couturiers—particularly Lacroix and Ungaro—and almost overnight delivered their designs to the stores at very reasonable prices. This time Costa is in dark glasses, leaning against the museum wall and swinging his satchel, which I am sure is full of design goodies from other shows that have already been facsimiled back to Texas, where busy Mexican hands are sewing up all of Paris.

We have forgotten Costa by the time Emanuel Ungaro comes down the runway among his dressed-to-kill but exotic mannequins—as exotic as the Datura, that poisonous flower that hangs limp all day, then perks up at night and gives out an aphrodisiacal scent that has been known to cause hallucinations. And that's what we write in *WWD* about the Ungaro collection, and we hope Monsieur Ungaro understands we are praising it, because, after all, that Datura is a powerful plant and Ungaro is the most exotic of the designers.

. . .

Never to be outdone and always trying the outrageous, Kaiser (our nickname for him), Karl Lagerfeld is about to show his Chanel collection in the newly redecorated Théâtre des Champs Élysées, and we are all very comfortable except for the French prime minister's wife, Michèle Rocard, who will not sit in the same theater box with Princess Caroline of Monaco, who is there with her husband who is clutching a small dog. Is it the dog or the Monaco couple? Who knows? The French can be difficult when it comes to "placement."

Strong hands grip my shoulders just before the show starts. Alain Wertheimer, the young owner of Chanel, whispers to me, "Bohan is finished at Dior." Before I can ask him what is happening to Karl at Chanel, where Lagerfeld is paid more than $1 million a year, Wertheimer moves quickly away to his seat. I do not see him again and can't reach him after the show.

The Lagerfeld show for Chanel begins on a wide-open stage flanked by two grand pianos. A young man with slicked-down hair and painted red lips swishes onto the stage. We all wonder what he is doing there, especially since he is wearing shiny satin breeches, white knee socks and rows of Chanel chains around his waist. Has Karl gone mad? Now the man on stage starts singing in a high soprano voice, as the Chanel chains quiver. He keeps singing while the first models, in long skirts with short jackets, move up and down the steps. According to the program accompanying the show, Karl is taking us back to Shakespeare, but when, days after the show, we ask him, "Why a male singer with a high soprano voice?" Karl sputters his answer. "Oh, I couldn't put a female singer on the stage with the models. They would have torn a female to bits. Do you know that high voice is real? Loiseleur des Longchamps [the unlikely name of the singer] hasn't been castrated. Everyone thinks so, but he hasn't. He took down his pants in front of his girlfriends to prove it." We can't ask Karl another thing after that.

. . .

At Dior, Marc Bohan has always made it his business to pack in the celebrities. His favorite and certainly the favorite of the photographers is that same Princess Caroline of Monaco. As she and her husband, Stefano, assail the wall of photographers, their bodyguard almost loses control. It always amuses me to see her entrance because the other women in the front row glare jealously as she finally sits down. She smiles demurely and says not one word to her husband, who is again wearing his six-button linen vest (I have never seen a vest quite like it). He looks straight ahead, almost ashamed to be at a fashion show. Princess Caroline and the family are said to sell lots of magazines— especially *Paris Match* and *Jour de France*—and rumor has it they have paying contracts to model, babies and all, at their discretion.

At Dior I am sitting next to Marianne Bohan, Marc's daughter, who is in there rooting for her father. As the show progresses and the perky suits with short jackets and the full swinging mohair coats pass, we all feel good vibes in the room. When it is over, Marc Bohan, who has been designing longer than almost any other designer in Paris, at age sixty-one has a triumph—his best collection so far. How important and how wonderful for him. Marc doesn't know as he comes down the runway to thunderous applause that Karl Lagerfeld has been spreading the word around Paris that Bohan's contract at Dior is up and that Lagerfeld will leave Chanel to take over Dior. We check carefully, and the rumor is vigorously denied. And afterward Lagerfeld admits that he floated his move to Dior just to add a little juicy gossip "to the season." Or was it just to sweeten his yearly contract with Chanel? Who knows?

We hope that Marc Bohan, who has been battered around for years, will come out unscathed again, because in his almost forty years in fashion, he has had his ups and downs.

Bohan tells us during dinner outside in the Ritz Espadon garden (one of the great joys of eating in Paris) how when he was a bank clerk at the Banque de Paris Nord he would sneak into the couture shows during his lunch break. His first sketches were accepted at the house of Piquet when he was only nineteen; then he went to Molyneux (his style is still Molyneux in spirit). In 1953 he opened his own couture house, which closed six months later. He was head designer at Patou for four years before he went to Dior to replace Yves Saint Laurent after the director of Dior "let" Saint Laurent be drafted (Saint Laurent's second collection was deemed not commercial enough for the great Dior machine). Marc Bohan gave the house of Dior just what they wanted—conventional blousing shirtwaist dresses—and was such a success that he was pushed out onto the Dior balcony as traffic on the avenue Montaigne stopped, a crowd gathered, and he was the king of Paris fashion for that day.

Bohan, along with Saint Laurent, has dressed more women than any other Paris designer. Still he lives more simply than his fellow designers. In addition to a small apartment, he has a country house near Fontainebleau, where he does all his own cooking. He is the only designer I know who mounts a horse and gallops through the forest on weekends. About his "only folly," to use his words, is a small château on the edge of Burgundy, which will "take the rest of my life and my money" to arrange.

When Bohan left Dior, he received a settlement of more than $2 million, and he looked like a million himself, even though he told me sadly, "This will be the first time in thirty years that I will not be doing a collection." Then he added, "But I'm sure I will be back."

. . .

No couture season can end without the Yves Saint Laurent collection. As usual Paris was rife that July of '88 with rumors that Saint Laurent wasn't well and that the collection was not finished. As it turned out the collection had never been so ready. He had started work in May and he had a surprise for everyone, for his way of working had totally changed.

We were the first to preview just a small part of the collection: one model showing a *smoking* coat (inspired by a man's tuxedo) and under it a skirt and blouse. We were standing on the Champs Élysées with the hairdresser and three young women from Saint Laurent here to observe that the master's work was in no way distorted. The Champs Élysées was lined with tricolor flags. We put the model on the curb and Philippe photographed her in every position so that when the *smoking* came out on a full page in *W* you could see Saint Laurent was right when he said that one model was "the essence of my collection." It was like old times: *WWD/W* were seeing the collection first. And we could tell from just this one model that Saint Laurent was still the King of Fashion. Would his show confirm our first great impression?

The day of the show we all expect Madame Mitterrand to be there and she is. I am just entering the grand salon of the Hotel Intercontinental when a strong arm pushes me aside and I turn to see a woman bodyguard making her way through the crowd followed by the first lady of France, all in white. Danielle Mitterrand's eyes penetrate everything in her sight as she serenely takes her place. She is unsmiling until Pierre Bergé, head of the house of Saint Laurent, hears she is there and rushes down the runway to embrace her. Bergé, who in size and stance could be a stand-in for Napoleon, is not only close to Madame Mitterrand but is a big supporter of her husband.

The room is packed with all those other celebrities who worship the King of Fashion. There is Catherine Deneuve, who looks "plainly beautiful," sitting next to Madame Mitterrand, who sits next to her sister-in-law, who sits next to Monique Lang, wife of the Minister of Culture, who is sitting next to me. Around the inner circle, Hélène Rochas, Betty Catroux (Saint Laurent's closest friend), Paloma Picasso and her husband, who changes his dark glasses for every show. And way down in the second row, Yves Saint Laurent's mother, who is over seventy and looks younger than most of the other women dressed by her son.

The King's court is present and he is ready to show that he is still very much on the fashion throne. Because we were banned from his last couture show, we from *WWD/ W* have mixed feelings. When one has fought with a friend of more than thirty years, a friend whose career really paralleled ours in the old days, it is emotional to be sitting there hoping now that Saint Laurent and Fairchild Publications can move ahead together again.

From the time YSL was dismissed from Dior in the late '50s, he and we were joined at the hip in our two careers. When he opened his own couture house, we respected and supported him. We were severely, and rightfully so, criticized during the '80s for raving about his collections when his fashion influence was slipping. We were wrong sometimes, but I just could not get it out of my mind that Chanel and then Saint Laurent were the designers of our century, and would probably never be surpassed in their fashion power.

Our worshiping at the altar of Saint Laurent came to an end when, after his couture show in July 1987, we were lukewarm in our review. What made matters worse was that, some months later, he showed his Rive Gauche collection and we wrote it up not on the first page as usual but on page 16 of *WWD*. We used the first page and a double page in color for Christian Lacroix—a real scoop because everyone was waiting to see what he would do in ready-to-wear.

It was too much for the great house of YSL to bear. So they banned us from all the shows and Saint Laurent activities. We carried little news and no fashion about Saint Laurent for almost a year.

When respect and friendship are ruptured after thirty years, it takes great patience and effort to pick up the broken pieces, but we tried—amidst intrigue between YSL and *WWD* that was as convoluted as that in the Russian court of the czars. We spent $10,000 preparing a leather-bound book containing all that *W* and *WWD* had written over the years about Saint Laurent. The book was so heavy it took a strong messenger to deliver it to Saint Laurent's Left Bank home. We never got an acknowledgment.

Our feud became news. Pierre Bergé, YSL's partner in this operatic drama, called me a megalomaniac in an article that appeared on the front page of the *International Herald Tribune.* Agence France Presse asked me what I thought about being called a megalomaniac. My response: "I have respect for YSL's talent." The war continued, the fashion establishment and the fashion press enjoying every moment of the battle, until finally Saint Laurent and Bergé had had enough and put us back on their invitation list.

But when Bergé issued the invitation, he said to me, "Now we will see what you write." We made no deals. It was just common sense that brought us back together, common sense and mutual respect.

We are happy to be back, especially happy when we see that Saint Laurent is giving us his best collection of all the fifty-three he has created over the years. Close to perfect: the suit jackets cut in his strict style but the skirts softened with pleats. And his colors—he is the master of color in fashion—are equal to those in a Matisse painting. (His clothes are often inspired by painters: Mondrian, Picasso, Braque, and Matisse.) He brings down the house when he starts showing his twenty-two *smokings* of coats, suits, and skirts. As one of the last *smokings* approaches Madame Mitterrand, she breaks into a big smile, for Saint Laurent has had the French Legion of Honor red ribbon sewn onto the lapel.

Then, in typical Saint Laurent fashion, there is a change of pace. Out come evening jackets, richly embroidered in life-size fruits. There is a standing ovation. I look over at Saint Laurent's mother, and she is serene, but next to her, Gustav Zumsteg, who designed many of the fabrics for Saint Laurent over the years, is in tears. With the finale to the music of *Turandot,* the King comes down the runway with his bride clutching lilies. As they reach the end of the runway he has his model kneel and her lilies touch his green velvet jacket with their orange stain.

By the time we manage to fight our way backstage, Saint Laurent is surrounded by television lights, cameras, and women frantically trying to reach him. His face is smeared with lipstick. As we wait, I am thinking of what I am going to say. Then suddenly he breaks through the crowd with his two bodyguards pushing ahead, and, led by Pierre Bergé, he embraces me so strongly I think my neck is wrenched. He whispers in my ear, "Thank you, thank you for coming. I'm glad the war is all over—so glad. Let's never mention it again." And I tell him: "You will never be able to do a collection as great as this again." Saint Laurent: "I know, but I am so happy."

Two days after his triumph, I go to see Saint Laurent in his castle, 55 rue de Babylone, right in the center of Paris. Through the courtyard and up the stairs to the glass Art Deco door: I push the doorbell while a small television camera watches. The door opens and a young Moroccan servant in a red jacket lets me in. A vase of red roses, another of yellow, are in the middle of the entrance hall, sent to Saint

Laurent to celebrate his collection. Down the hall, the grand salon looks dark but the smell of lilies fills the room, which is dominated by precious objects, most precious of all a Goya painting of a little boy with a ruffled lace collar. The light from the garden seeps through, and beyond the garden is a forest of trees. The door opens and Yves Saint Laurent walks slowly through it and puts his arms around me.

"I am so glad you are here again. I know you like it downstairs in the library; let's go down there." We go down the winding dark stairway, led by Moujik, his French bulldog. Saint Laurent stops for a moment by a huge Buddha watched over by a collection of cameos in carefully lit elegant cases. Down in the white room, Lalanne's life-size sculpted sheep graze. Lying on the floor are four of Warhol's last portraits: they are all of Moujik, who is now also spread out on the floor.

"I am happy, so happy with my success," says Saint Laurent, lowering his head. Long pause. "Yes, I am alone, the King in his Castle. I want to be alone, except for a few friends." The only one he mentions is Betty Catroux. "I want to be alone," he repeats. "I am happy this way," and he turns his head and again looks at the floor. "All I need is a crayon in my hand just to sketch. That gives me joy. I never go out, not even to the movies, rarely to a restaurant. And I don't want to be with the rich or with society. Never. I do help the young doctors at the Hospital de Paris, and if they need something I try and give it to them, like television sets.

"My real love is my house, my couture house. They are all wonderful, so wonderful. In two seconds I can show my *directrices* of ateliers a new model and right away they understand perfectly."

Does the heavy responsibility of making a new collection every three months weigh on his shoulders?

A long sigh and Saint Laurent reaches for a cigarette. "Agony, agony, always agony. When I get up in the morning I walk around doing nothing. Putting it off. Waiting to go to the office. And the only reason I go there is Moujik." He points to the dog, who is snoring. "He loves the maison couture, so I have to go. He gets me there. I go frightened of what I have to do. I go very late. But when I am there I am happy because of all my people. They are the best. Together we have almost succeeded in creating the perfect. We have arrived at that point in technique. We have the best fashion hands in the world. I know."

Back to Moujik. "He is always with me, by my side, never moving when I am sick. But when I get mad or there is trouble, he goes away. He just doesn't like any trouble. That's why he loves to go to the couture house."

Now Saint Laurent is looking straight ahead and I can see the glow in his eyes through his glasses. "You know this collection was quite extraordinary. For the first time, way back in April, I made every sketch in every color of every design—jewels, hats, shoes, belts, fabrics. They were sketches in full detail and we worked strictly from these and barely changed anything. My ateliers love to work from these originals because they can see the dress finished before their eyes. I did all these sketches upstairs in the room next to my bedroom where no one is allowed to go. I feel so secure within these walls all alone. That is where I work. And, no, you can't go in there, it is such a mess."

I ask him about his relationship with Pierre Bergé, who has been appointed by Mitterrand as the director of the Paris Opera, and responsible as well for the new opera house at the Bastille. But I don't bring up the subject of Bergé's appointment, which has stirred enormous publicity and controversy, because Bergé made me promise not to. I know Saint Laurent is jealous, and I think to myself that he and Bergé are like two divas.

Saint Laurent, too, avoids the subject. "Oh, Pierre," he says. "You know he is much calmer. I now understand we could not live together under one roof. It is much better now, so much better. For eight years I was very bad, very bad. It was a difficult period. Pierre was wonderful, really wonderful to me. I can never forget. Now that it is calm, we have a fine friendship."

When Saint Laurent and I first became friends, he described himself to me as "being born with a nervous breakdown." Now I ask him about his health—and especially about his drinking.

"Well, the doctor, a great specialist, has spent hours examining me and told me afterward there was nothing wrong that he could find. And then when I was so sick he told me that he had never seen anyone so strong, or anyone make such a quick recovery. I am better now. I will be frank. I do still drink, but less. And believe it or not, I have lost weight. I used to be out to there, way out." He stretches his legs, and ashes from his cigarette fall to the floor, spraying his white pinwale corduroy slacks. He kicks the ashes away with his thin suede desert boots, then carefully adjusts his yellow handkerchief in his pocket.

"Is it necessary for me to go to New York? I don't think so. What would it prove? I love America but New York is too hard for me, especially now. I want to stay here in my castle and work, just like an old Leo. [Saint Laurent was fifty-two on August 1.] I could take painting lessons. I understand that with a good professor in three months I could learn perspective. You know I cheat in my sketches; they aren't exactly right. I should learn."

And fashion? "We don't want to talk about that. In this collection I love every dress so much, every model, every fabric. I love to see and touch the girls when I am fitting on them. Of course, I have made refinements in my clothes. The new pleated skirts on my suits. No one could do that except Coco Chanel. I saw her across a room a long time ago. But I told Pierre I didn't want to meet her—ever. I was afraid to. She was a sorcière. And so old at the end. And alone, so alone. Like me doing our work."

So ended another high-fashion season in the highest court of fashion. But there is always a new one. Less than three months after Marc Bohan was dismissed from the House of Dior, Gianfranco Ferré is ensconced in his Dior studio with its wood floors and all white, modern, slick Italian chic, with not a trace of the Dior past. And we are there to see the first Gianfranco Ferré model to come out of one of Paris's most powerful fashion houses.

Rita Airaghi, Ferré's right arm, has tears in her eyes. The directress of Dior, the official photographer, the tailor, the press attaché are all there as we prepare to shoot the cover for *W*. Ferré marches into the room followed by his newborn Dior—a coat and dress in Ferré red (his trademark: a perfect blend of red and orange) worn by a very large model in a small top hat. We place Ferré on a Louis XVI armchair that was in the office of the late Christian Dior. We stand the girl next to Ferré, who is seated in front of two white fitting dummies. I cannot help thinking the dummies are the ghosts of Marc Bohan and Yves Saint Laurent, Ferré's predecessors at Dior. (Ironically, just the day before, Saint Laurent's stock offering of 400,000 shares was on the Paris Bourse—the first time for a couture house. Enthusiastic buyers placed orders for 103,641,000—270 times over. What a tribute to Saint Laurent and the power of fashion.)

Ferré tells us his simple philosophy: "I love my work. I love my life." But when asked how he feels about following the great Dior, he responds: "I have looked at all his sketches and all the special clothes he made for the world's elegant women. In the beginning the sketches were gentle, at the end of his final, tenth year you could see in his drawings an unhappy, tormented man." In Ferré's eyes you can see that he can imagine it happening to him.

10
SAVAGE FASHION

There are still many women who will pay as much as $26,000 for a Paris dress. Winging their way across the Atlantic to buy their clothes for the season are Ivana Trump and her group, aboard the Trumps' private Boeing 727. In the group is Nan Kempner, a New Yorker transplanted from San Francisco, who has never missed an important party. On this trip, Mrs. Kempner will help "introduce Mrs. Trump" to some couture houses and will arrange friendly invitations to the smart parties taking place during the Paris showings.

Mrs. Kempner, who is lean, athletic, and nice, just loves clothes. She travels the couture circuit from New York to Rome to Paris, buying clothes and arranging special prices, hoping she'll be photographed wearing a Saint Laurent, Valentino, or some other designer's dress. Anything goes for free publicity, and few designers mind seeing their clothes paraded through the papers—especially through *WWD*. We have taken to not photographing Mrs. Kempner simply because she throws herself in front of the camera, living up to the deals she cuts with many designers, going everywhere, making the scene on two continents.

Designers in the fashion horse race are not opposed to making special "arrangements" for important women who will be seen wearing their clothes at the right places. The one woman designers want to dress is Jacqueline Onassis. For a while, Mrs. O. wore Valentino and we received calls from Valentino's Rome office, telling us things like "Jackie will wear such-and-such tomorrow." After a while, however, fashion editors grew tired of showing even Mrs. Onassis in her Valentinos. But when she shifted to wearing Caroline Herrera, it became news all over again.

In the long run, it's better for a designer to dress different people, never to get boxed in by one personality. Though Jackie Onassis still commands the respect of all designers, she seems to have lost the kind of interest in clothes that she once had. More and more, she stays out of the New York limelight. When I saw her last November at the New York Public Library's Literary Lions party, standing there with Maurice Tempelsman, she looked exasperated by all the fuss and seemed almost lost in the throng of her social peers.

Wearing the latest from Paris does not necessarily mean that rich and social ladies look their best. The woman in the dress is more important than the dress she's wearing. Fashion is only a minor accessory to any woman's beauty. What really counts is her charm. Many a woman has become a fashion victim, even though her new clothes come from Paris. No one has to spend a fortune to be well dressed —they only have to wear what they enjoy and what feels right.

But if a fashion victim feels better for spending the price of a small garage on one dress, let her be. Fashion is not solely in the eyes of the beholder, but in the eyes of the wearer as well.

There's no need, then, for a woman to take off for Paris unless she really gets her kicks spending a great deal of money to wear a Paris original. She might find the same dress modified for her needs in a store right in her own backyard. Of course, the dress won't have the same quality of workmanship, and the fabric might not be the same. But even the woman who pays thousands for a dress has to go through the difficult process of trying to find out what suits her, not what is just the latest fashion. Sometimes it's fashionable to be unfashionable, important not to follow "the trends."

Talking of trends. On a recent plane ride I realized that ninety percent of the passengers were wearing sneakers. They looked like Minnie and Mickey Mouse. The few men and women in leather shoes really had some style—simply because they were *not* following the crowd. This is not to say that sneakers aren't practical and, most of all, comfortable, but being comfortable is not enough.

So who's to say what one should and should not wear? There really aren't any authorities and no one—expert or not—should tell you what is right to wear or what is fashionable.

We have a friend, the Marquis Robert de Goulaine, who lives at the Château de Goulaine, Haute Goulaine, Basse Goulaine, France. (It is such a noble address, I couldn't resist recording it.) He too feels that you can know much about people from looking at what shoes they wear in airports. He says the English at Heathrow wear "sad shoes" and the Americans and the French "happy shoes." Maybe, then, sneakers are a happy shoe after all, because they stand for action, sport, and the outdoors. That's probably why so many people in the world wear them—because they want to be comfortable and to look alive. In addition, sneakers are classless.

In the past, sneakers would never have been acceptable except on the tennis court. Today, almost any fashion goes anywhere. Who would have imagined that blue jeans could be worn with a tuxedo jacket, or that cowboy boots could look right with a business suit? Ralph Lauren has more than fifty pairs of cowboy boots in his New York closet. The late Françoise de la Renta walked all over New York in a four-ply cashmere turtleneck sweater, a black Saint Laurent skirt—and white sneakers. Even Susan Gutfreund strolls through Central Park on Sundays with John, Jr., in an old raincoat and sneakers. But she would never walk down the rue de Grenelle in Paris in sneakers. Never. The elegant Frenchwomen have not yet arrived at this relaxed point. The Americans are way ahead in real fashion.

Sometimes "throw-away chic" worn by the right woman can outstyle the best of high fashion. I remember standing outside the Ritz Hotel on the rue Cambon very late one night in the pouring rain with Coco Chanel. I don't remember what she was talking about, but I remember that she wore her old raincoat tied smartly to one side. It was chic. So is the way Yves Saint Laurent wears his pocket handkerchief at just the right angle. Chanel and Saint Laurent have that alluring combination of style and chic born in them. Style is part of you or it isn't. You can't buy it.

We live in an era when all generations are increasingly conscious of style. People strive for it by wearing status symbols, as much as to say, "Here I am, a member of the Chic Club, and I can afford to belong." But some who pay thousands of dollars never make the club at all, while some executive assistant in her snappy little gray flannel suit decorated with a Hermès scarf truly looks chic.

To put all the cards on the table, I would have to say that the women who look the best, day in and day out, are the Americans. They have what I would call slick chic: they are well groomed, their hair is clean, their clothes are well tailored and they are simply dressed. Sometimes their fashions lack character, but they are always pleasant to look at. (An exception to this exists in one of America's richest communities, Greenwich, Connecticut. There, to be "just one of the girls," you have to go out in hair curlers that are barely covered by an old scarf. Conforming in Greenwich is the reverse of chic, still another way of being a fashion victim.)

Working women (how I hate those words "working women") often steal the show with their style. I am not talking about the kind of career dressing characterized by "uniforms" resembling a man's suit. I'm referring to those women who through their travels in large cities know just how to put themselves together. In the final analysis, they win out with their brains and beauty. If a woman is smart in business and also has style, she's way ahead of men and other women.

To me, next to a woman's beauty and charm (and, I have to admit meekly, the way that she dresses) her greatest asset is an attitude that says: "Go ahead and try it. We will succeed." It's true of the women I know in business and it's especially true of my wife. Women are, in every sense, a creative force. Men are not as daring ("Oh, we've never done that before!").

European women, especially Frenchwomen, win hands down for their intelligence in their relationships with men. Deep down they control their men, letting them run free up to a point, then exerting their charm and beauty to see that they stay in line. And Frenchmen, as my wife, Jill, puts it simply, "make a woman feel like a woman." How? I jealously keep asking.

"He kisses her hand. He flirts. He pays attention to her. He just makes her feel great," I'm told.

But now it's my turn, so let's get back to the Frenchwoman. First of all, she doesn't want to look or act like every other woman. She is in competition with other women. The French want to be individuals at all costs. A Frenchwoman is really concerned with how she looks. She's an object of desire, not just a housewife or a working woman. For me, one of the most beautiful of women—and I am talking about sheer beauty, ageless beauty—is Hélène Rochas, who has the good fortune to be in the beauty business. Just look at her eyes, her skin, her posture, her Saint Laurent clothes. You would never guess that Madame Rochas is over sixty. She deserves the title we gave her: "Queen of Beauty." And with all her native beauty, she is very much part of that Paris world of style. Why not? She enjoys it.

Why do we follow trends? Why do almost all of us, men and women, want to be the same as others we admire? Perhaps many of us are just born to be copycats.

Why are certain people and certain things in or out? When we at *W* invented the In and Out list, it was not just for the hell of it but because there is no question that people talk about the ins and outs of society, fashion, places, things, living, and even of each other. We live in a time when we are preoccupied with what is hot and what is cold, what is black, what is white. The tepid, the gray seem to have disappeared from our thoughts.

In defense of *W*'s annual In and Out list, I should say that we are not out merely to sell newspapers, although that's part of it. What it all comes down to is fashion. The age of plenty gives people the time, energy, and money to indulge in this game of Ins and Outs. Unfortunately, the In-and-Out crowd sometimes travels a bumpy road. We are the most guilty of the In-and-Outers, because we are stuck with counting Ins and Outs in our sleep, and sometimes we start an avalanche. One advertiser, a leading Swiss watch manufacturer—a big one—canceled all his advertising with us when we put his famous watch on the Out list. Other Swiss watch manufacturers got together and followed, canceling major ad campaigns in *W*.

What's In and Out has a logical beginning and ending. From all outward appearances, Nancy Reagan, with her fashion and her parties, transformed the White House from the days of the "Plain Carters" into an elegant "palace." Even the most cynical Europeans came away from Reaganesque state dinners and private parties raving about the flowers, the food, the service, the entertainment. They hadn't sounded like that since the days of Jacqueline Kennedy. Most White House guests, however, did not say they had a "stimulating" time or even that they had fun, and there were numerous negative comments about the bizarre guest lists. Maybe you just can't win in the White House.

When she became First Lady, Nancy Reagan said she would wear only American clothes, but when in the spring of 1989 she went to Paris with the former President (on the private jet of Saudi Arabian Mouaffak Al-Midani) to celebrate the hundredth anniversary of the Eiffel Tower, Nancy went on a shopping spree at Givenchy. For all the parties she attended in Paris, she wore Valentino, and the designer flew up from Rome to be with her. The last time French President François Mitterrand saw the Reagans was at one of their farewell private dinners at the White House. Mitterrand was seated to the right of Nancy, and to her left was someone I have promised to call "an unnamed fashion designer." The president of France talked for two hours to former ambassador Jeane Kirkpatrick while Nancy talked to her designer. There is no doubt about it: the former First Lady loves her designers.

But new trends depend on the moods of the moment. Now that the Reagans are gone, California's Nouvelle Society (Bloomingdale, Annenberg, and company) obviously will be less in evidence and the Eastern social and intellectual establishment will take over. The Hollywood glamour of the Reagan White House will be replaced by no-nonsense Eastern Ivy League Waspiness, which I hope will not be boring. We Wasps do tend to be stuffy. The fashion and elegance of the last eight years will be downplayed. For the moment, glamour has been snuffed out at the White House.

This change to a more no-fashion mood doesn't mean that Barbara Bush will dress and entertain badly. It means she will do her job her way and in her style. Great.

Barbara Bush's way is not anti-fashion. After all, she spends time and money dressing at Bill Blass in a way suitable to her. I cannot see her overly concerned with her clothes or see a Zipkin-type Walker calling almost daily on her private line or helping her with her wardrobe. Nor will a decorator be brought in to redo the White House private quarters. At least not right away. The Bushes' hearts belong to the rolling, foggy, bracing seas of Maine.

At this moment, the no-chichi, almost anti-chic attitude of the Bushes happens to reflect the mood of the country. We see falling interest in fashion, bad store sales in all fashion except accessories. Oddly enough, when you hear store executives talking about fashion, they say men are becoming more fashion-conscious than women. George Bush, however, will never give up his Ivy League loafers for those sleek, slim Italian shoes.

People don't change, not even presidents, and there's no reason why George and Barbara Bush should, just because they are in that goldfish bowl called the White House. I'm sure an invitation to the White House will be just as cherished as before. I'm also sure those four or five high priestesses of Washington society will be less critical of the

Bushes than they were of the Carters and even of the Reagans, because for years the Bushes have been in the inner circle of hard-core Georgetown society. The White House will be more relaxed and less inflexibly elegant than before. New England (with Texas touches), here we come. Goodbye, California; hello, Eastern-style society.

My memories of the Bushes go back more than ten years to the time when we visited them in the People's Republic of China when George Bush was head of the U.S. liaison office there. We saw firsthand how the Bushes lived: simply, but graciously. They like each other's company and being with a few friends.

I remember a day in China when Jill and I were racing through Peking with George and Barbara Bush in their limousine. George Bush turned to us very seriously and said how proud he was to represent our country and that it gave him a thrill to see the Stars and Stripes flying from the fender.

Our last time with the Bushes was on a bright sunny afternoon, again in Peking. The Marine guards at their official residence had been looking all over Peking for them: President Ford was calling. The Bushes had gone to church on their bicycles. Ford wanted to tell Bush he was to be head of the CIA. Good soldier that he was, Bush accepted the position immediately. But Barbara had tears in her eyes as she said, "I cannot believe it. We have to move again for the fifth time in less than ten years."

Just before the election Barbara Bush gave an exclusive interview to *WWD/W*. Susan Watters, bureau chief of the Washington office, produced a graphic portrait of the woman who was to become the new First Lady: "I think I'm at peace with myself. I don't think I've always been. I'm still feisty." And warm and motherly.

"She's one of those ladies of a certain age—competent Episcopal ladies, the backbone of the community," says Chris Buckley, a former Bush speechwriter, "the kind of women who make the car pools run. Ladies who—if there were a crisis—come into their own and are magnificent. In a Bush administration you'd see her at the bedside of every national calamity. She'd hold our hand."

Jeb Bush, her son, describes her as the "captain" and the mother always in charge. Fashion and objects take a back seat to people and her family. About her only comment on fashion to Susan Watters, as she sat in a simple suit from Bill Blass, with a double strand of pearls and girlish pink nail polish, was: "I was looking at my clothes the other day and wishing I saw some more color."

Her entertaining style has always been a relaxed one with buffet dinners. And when public office is over, Mrs. Bush dreams of spending more time in her garden on Walker Point, Kennebunkport, Maine.

"I'm a nester and that house means roots. When I'm in my garden in Maine, putting in peonies that will last a hundred years in the ground, I'm planting for generations. I'm doing that for my children and grandchildren." Yes, the White House is going to be a very different place—an Ivy League house presided over by a strong mother. And we all need a mother, don't we?

The change in mood and ideas from Reagan to Bush has already affected fashion—temporarily. Fashion is now at a standstill, slow period with little or no excitement. All is quiet after the pouf explosion of Christian Lacroix. But it won't be long before the fashion wheel comes back to the wild and the savage. We are returning to the fiery independence of the sixties. No one, especially the young, can remain bored for long. The wheel of fashion never stops turning. Consumers become restless. From thinking of the house, their nesting place, they go back to the fun-and-games of self-indulgent fashion that takes them out of the home and more into themselves. There is our answer to the Ins and Outs—there is no way to understand or predict the ways of fashion. All we know is that it appeals to the most savage instincts in all of us. The tribal dance continues and the big chief fashion designers beat their drums just to survive in that jungle.

A good designer has to look everywhere for a new idea. Imagine yourself locked in a dark, dreary studio high above Seventh Avenue. Even with the air conditioning whirring away you can hear the traffic and the frenzy of the avenue way below. They call it "Fashion Avenue," which is a joke: it's one of the ugliest streets in the city. And you are stuck with that nasty problem—you have to stay in business and sell a product line at a better price than the designer on the floor below you. Is he making something better? Have you got what the consumer wants or are you making dogs that will end up on the markdown rack? Your reputation is on the line. Designers must live with their egos and with what society and the press are saying about them. Designers hang on to their success by a thread. Only some of the gang really have staying power. Claude Montana's staying power is the fact that his workmanship is unsurpassed. His coats, sweaters, and suits have made him the superman of quality sportswear. The blond French cowboy uses Amazons for models of his big, powerful clothes.

The designers' game is dangerous and competitive. Many so-called observers and fashion experts (and there really are *no* fashion experts) have attempted to prove there is some sort of conspiracy in which all the designers get together in a secret meeting place and plot how to make women spend more money to buy their newest fashions. The whole concept is wrong. I still insist I have never met two designers who agree on anything concerning what they'll make. As a matter of fact, the game is so tough that designers guard their secrets with their lives. In Paris, the blinds are drawn tight at all the couture houses while collections are being "created." Only members of the staff are allowed into a studio. Still, secrets have a way of getting out. Some mannequins, for example, love to talk.

One designer at 550 Seventh Avenue used to know within twenty-four hours what Yves Saint Laurent was fitting. The descriptions he was given by the spy within the House of Saint Laurent couture were totally accurate. Saint Laurent became so concerned with spying he refused to let his private customers take home videos of the couture collection for fear they might fall into the hands of an American designer.

Every male designer needs to have a woman in his creative life. There are few top designers in Paris or the United States (Californian James Galanos is an exception) who do not have women right next to them in the studio. The warmth, charm, and good common sense of women are essential to the creation of important fashion—it takes a woman to judge what a woman really will wear. Designers may not all share their beds with women, but they always value their opinions. Saint Laurent has his close friend, tall, blonde, trusted Betty Catroux, as well as his assistant, Madame Anne Marie Muñoz (a saint if ever there was one), and his gypsy muse, LouLou Klossowski. Ferré has five Italian women working with him in his Dior studio. Lacroix has his "mother"-inspirer, Françoise Roesenstiehl. Bill Blass has Laura Montalban. Blass has been fitting on her for twenty years and, as he says, they tug and pull, fight and yell, but they can do a collection together.

That master of women and fashion, Emanuel Ungaro, has a whole harem: Ariane Brener, Ariane Dandois and, at this writing, Laura Fanfani, who gave up her husband to be with him. Ungaro is another man from the South of France who has eyes that burn bright. He and Lacroix are two hypnotic magicians who create their own special kind of strong, earthy fashion inspired by the power and beauty of women.

America's most influential designer is a woman. Donna Karan is in the tradition of Madame Alix Grès, the great French couturière, who knew how to drape fabric to a woman's body. Karan is a master of body draping, so very important in making great fashion. She understands a woman's body better than her male rivals do. And she is also totally modern. Karan is America's Chanel. She is our best, even though, like all great designers, her concepts have European roots.

The first time I met Donna Karan, she took my hand and pulled me off my chair to show me how well her blazer fit the model. Surprisingly, those blazers she designs for women can fit men perfectly.

There is an all-male fashion designer who works without the help of women and stands almost alone in his own special world: Jean-Paul Gaultier. Sometimes Gaultier gives the impression that he is ridiculing both men and women by dressing them almost in the mood of Fellini. His designs are neuter—and almost out of another world. That does not mean he is not one of the forces in fashion. His style is just different. At times it strays from the normal to the odd seemingly for the sake of being odd. When I saw his models wearing bralike tops and garter belts, I felt distaste, for to me this was fashion bordering on the grotesque—like a show in some sleazy Hamburg bar. But then I'm a square, or so I'm constantly being told.

THE NOUVELLES
AND OTHERS

2

3

June 5, 1971: first dummy of *W*—a disaster (1).
April 7, 1972: Number 1, Volume 1—first issue of *W*
(2).
Hot pants: name came to me on IRT subway and
appears in Webster's Dictionary (3).

Bill Paley of CBS and his wife, Queen Babe, way before Nouvelle S
(1).
Jackie O. (2).
On the right, reigning queen of what's left of society—Marella Agne
and dashing, daring, brilliant Gianni Agnelli (3), with their inner cou
including Kim d'Estainville, Irith Landeau, Bill Paley, Annette Reed
Ascanio Branca. From left to right: Ascanio Branca, Annette Reed, M
Agnelli, Bill Paley, Irith Landeau, Kim d'Estainville, and Gianni Agn
(4).
Annette Reed and Gianni Agnelli (5). Sam Reed, Kim d'Estainville,
Annette Reed, Marella and Gianni Agnelli (6).

3

4

5

6

4

5

W "Originals" cover girls: Lady Diana Cooper playing with her dog
(1). Annette Reed curling up like a cat (2). Isabelle Eberstadt (3). The
King and Queen of Cosmetics, Leonard and Estée Lauder (4). Kay
Graham walking out of the Washington *Post* (5). The Queen of New
York, Brooke Astor, with Douglas Dillon (6). Pat Buckley with Lowey
(7) and with Bill Buckley (8) and with Malcolm Forbes (9). Slim Keith,
seeing eye of New York society (10).

8

9

10

1

4

Jayne Wrightsman and Lord George Weidenfeld (1), Susan and John Gutfreund (2), Gayfryd and Saul Steinberg (3).

Edmond and Lily Safra (4). They give silver caviar spoons as gifts to their dinner guests.

Shopping center magnate and Sotheby's Alfred Taubman with his wife, Judy (5), the former Miss Israel.

Social Cyclones: Ivana Trump before her redo, Georgette Mosbacher and Gayfryd Steinberg (6). Lynn Wyatt and Peter Glenville (7).

5

2

3

6

7

C arolyne Roehm, skiing and smiling and posing (1).
Her châlet inside and outside in Vail, Colorado (2).

1

2

4

5

Mercedes Kellogg with former husband, Francis (3). Mercedes Kellogg with new husband, Sid Bass (4). Sid Bass with former wife, Anne (5).
Donald Trump with Ivana (6). Anne Bass with choreographer and dancer Peter Martins (7). Social Cyclone of Cyclones Georgette Mosbacher with Secretary of Commerce Robert Mosbacher (8).

6

7

8

Nancy Kissinger (1). With Henry (2). With the late labrador, Tyler (3). Our headline "I wonder who's Kissinger now" appeared in *Time* magazine (4).

5

6

Marylou Whitney dressed like her poodle, Edelweiss (5).
Hubert and Isabelle d'Ornano on the sidewalks of New York (6).
At Hobe Sound, the quintessential Wasps Nathaniel Reed and matriarch Permelia (7).

7

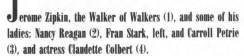

Jerome Zipkin, the Walker of Walkers (1), and some of his ladies: Nancy Reagan (2), Fran Stark, left, and Carroll Petrie (3), and actress Claudette Colbert (4).

Ashton Hawkins of the Metropolitan Museum. He walks and stocks the Met's war chest (5).
Intellectual Walker John Richardson with Nan Kempner (6).
Greek banker Alecko Papamarkou with Ann Getty (7). He sits at private White House dinners at the left of Nancy Reagan. He invests for the rich ladies he walks.

5

6

7

1

2

WWD troika: Fashion Editor Etta Froio with John Fairchild (1). President of Fairchild Group Michael Coady (2).
Patrick McCarthy, Fashion Group Vice-President and Associate Publisher of *Women's Wear Daily* and *W*, for the first time has his ears plugged (3).

4

6

5

7

October 1983: First issue of *M* (sister publication of *W*) with cover, Prince Philip (4). Readers did not know who he was.
October 1988: *M* cover "Greed"—a sellout (5).
August 1988: *M* cover "How Rich Is Rich"— another sellout (6).
Time magazine needlepoint cover of John Fairchild. Newsstand sales unknown (7).
Time cover © 1970 Time Inc. Reprinted by permission.

Fairchild with Roderick in Klosters,
Switzerland (1). *Photo by Jill Fairchild.*
Châlet Bianchina, the place we love (2).
Photo by Christopher Simon Sykes.
Courtesy HG.

11
AMERICAN SAVAGES

M ary McFadden, the first really big name from a
top-drawer social family to become an important designer, was about to descend upon us
at Mas Daumas, our country house near Me-
nebres in the South of France.

Her arrival was heralded by a telephone call
from the Sofitel Hotel at Marignan Airport
in Marseilles (hardly an In place for a Chic Savage like
McFadden to be resting her elegantly clipped head).
"John, is that you? I'm stranded, and I'm coming to you
for the night. Oscar gave me your number." Sometimes I

could kill Oscar de la Renta for arranging other people's lives.

In due course Mary arrived in a car she had rented for the occasion, bearing veritable Matterhorns of Vuitton suitcases and garment bags. It looked as if she planned to stay.

Her heart-wrenching tale moved me deeply. "My passport had expired, so the French pulled me off Cisneros's jet on the way to Mica's in Bodrum." (Translation: While en route to the home of Mica and Ahmet Ertegun, Mary had been involuntarily removed from the private jet of Gustavo Cisneros, a prominent Venezuelan tycoon.)

Mary, it turned out, had enjoyed herself immensely while sequestered at the Sofitel. The French authorities had been "charming," and to earn her bed and board she had been giving the other guests tennis and aerobics lessons.

"Just leave the bags in the car. I only need my makeup kit and that little one," she said, pointing to the luggage display in the back of the small Peugeot station wagon. "I'm just staying for the night. Then it's off to Bodrum in the morning."

What a night! For openers, Mary brought us up to date on her personal life. She told us that she had been married five times, "so far," and that her last husband had been a German with a beautiful body. "Not an ounce of fat; a real beauty."

Unhappily, according to Mary, number five was in Australia with most of her jewels and all the silver (he wasn't able to resist silver of any kind). But the real loves of her life, she went on during dinner—she ate nothing, but drank two glasses of white wine—were always older men, such as Lord George Weidenfeld, the British publisher, who is now a partner of Ann Getty in Wheatland Publishing. (Ann Getty is the statuesque, charity-minded wife of curly-haired Gordon Getty, who disappears into his music studio from

6:00 A.M. to 6:00 P.M. each day and writes operas, which are sometimes performed.)

By now we were in the living room, with Mary perched on the olive-green sofa under the large arch—a perfect setting for the continuation of her nonstop monologue. "I just love George. He is so intelligent. Everybody thinks so. Ann [Getty], Kay [Graham], Evangeline [Bruce], and Lally [Weymouth, Kay Graham's daughter]—they all love him. My mother [Mrs. Watson Blair] wanted me to marry him." (But her next marriage was again to a younger man.)

Here Mary paused to cop another nougat from the large bag sitting on the white-lacquered Chinese table. A strict diet built around white wine and candy?

What, I wondered, did so many famous women find so attractive about George Weidenfeld, who, for all his eminence, is decidedly on the corpulent side? (I looked down at my own bulging stomach. Mary couldn't abide that, and yet Mary was obsessed with Weidenfeld.) She went on:

"Of course, I proposed to George early on. At first he said no, but then he suggested he might reconsider if I would buy him a lovely country house."

"What do you see in him?" I just couldn't stop myself.

"Power plus intelligence. He knows about everything, and he is so exciting to be with. And he offers such superb advice on business and personal things. You should go to Israel with him, John. Visit Jerusalem; it's one of the most beautiful places in the world."

From Mary's point of view, we could not get enough of Lord George. She continued: "I loved every moment with him. Five minutes in his bedroom, and he sent me to bed, saying, 'We will meet only for breakfast.' "

It was growing late, and I realized that I had left the water running in the courtyard and garden. I dashed outside, loath to miss anything. But she was still at it when I returned, and the talk was still about sex.

"I'm supercautious now," she said. "I never go anywhere without my Dartmouth Sex Kit."

"What's a Dartmouth Sex Kit?" I asked, feeling terribly square.

"You don't know?" She looked at me in astonishment. "It has everything to protect you. Some students at Dartmouth invented it: special moistened, fleshlike condoms, a protective suit to prevent touching any open spots on the body, and, most important, a helmet."

I realized that I was being put on. (But still, I couldn't wait until the next day, after Mary had departed, to pass the story on to New York.)

Now Mary got down to her real point. "You know, John, this AIDS thing is a scourge. People are dying like flies. I've lost two assistants. The other day I went to yet another funeral, and all the boys were there. When they kissed me, I turned my cheek to the side so they wouldn't touch my skin, only my hair.

"It's so tragic, and it's dangerous to all of us," she went on. "I'm sure in five years we will only be seeing women designers. There won't be very many men left in fashion. You'll see."

A sobering thought, and not out of the realm of possibility, I suppose. Perry Ellis was one of the first of the top American designers to die of AIDS, and at the time, 1986, Michael Coady, who has worked with me as copublisher of *WWD/W* for fifteen years, observed that the whole fashion industry might be wiped out.

(I think the final word on the subject of homosexuality in the fashion industry came from the late Christian Dior. At the pinnacle of his success, in April 1950, he sailed into New York harbor on the *Queen Elizabeth,* and at a shipside press conference a reporter asked him: "Why are you and so many designers not married?" Though he was a shy man, Dior answered: "A man's personal life is his own.

What I do in my work is important; nothing else is the business of others. Thank you, gentlemen." The interview was over.)

Early the next morning, Mary donned a tight metallic jogging suit, stepped out into the garden at Mas Daumas, next to our 150-year-old olive tree, and took off down the dusty, rocky road. Forgoing breakfast, she departed right after her run in order to catch up with the de la Renta group, which included art expert and writer John Richardson; Boaz Mazor, salesman to Oscar's rich clients; Mercedes Kellogg, who had just left her husband for Sid Bass; and New York society princess Annette Reed and her super-Wasp husband, Samuel P. Reed.

Also in the de la Renta entourage were Kim d'Estainville, the handsome French part-time businessman, courtier to Italian billionaire Giovanni (Gianni) Agnelli of Fiat and his wife, Marella; and Lady Grace Dudley, a statuesque Yugoslav, now a British citizen, who lives in Switzerland and heads the Savage Set's CIA.

I found my thoughts going back to January 1963, when Oscar had first come to New York. Evil tongues were saying that after picking up pins for couturier Antonio del Castillo at Lanvin, he had crossed the Atlantic and become *de* la Renta. Not true, Oscar assured me; the *de* was part of his family name.

IIe told me that in 1955, at the age of eighteen, he had left his native Dominican Republic for Spain, thinking that he wanted to be a painter. In New York, en route, he started to work at Elizabeth Arden and was an instant success. It was during that time that he met Mary McFadden, and I can still see the two of them holding hands, sitting on the grass at our house in New Canaan, Connecticut. It was one of the first romances between a man designer and a woman designer, and even though Mary was just beginning her career, both would go on to become fashion stars—de

la Renta, a true social lion of New York. It was really
back then that the seeds of Nouvelle Society took root and
grew.

Not long thereafter, Gloria Vanderbilt, bearer of one of
the oldest social names in America, tossed away her white
gloves, lent her name to a line of blue jeans (imagine!), and
put the Vanderbilt swan on her perfume. Fashion as a
profession was at last becoming respectable in this country.
For a long time, Gloria had been painting and writing, but
she needed lots of money to support a luxurious life style.
As a result, she besieged fashion with a vengeance, traveling the length and breadth of America, cared for all the
while by her faithful maid, Nora, who unpacked the Vanderbilt sheets and pressed the Vanderbilt pillowcases for
her every night.

The first time I had a long talk with Gloria was at a dinner
at the home of Freddie Eberstadt, the son of a powerful investment banker. Isabelle and Freddie were the
toast of New York long before Nouvelle Society reared
its savage head. That night, Gloria, all in white lace, sat
gracefully on a large blue velvet sofa, talking to Andy
Warhol.

Jill and I were living in the same building as Gloria at the
time, 10 Gracie Square (evenings, when I returned home
from work, I used to see Gloria's makeup man going up in
the elevator to prepare her for her parties), so after the
Eberstadts' party, which Jill was unable to attend, Gloria
drove me home and invited me up to her penthouse, which
had belonged to conductor André Kostelanetz. She showed
me through the entire apartment, telling me about every
object, even to his Art Deco bathtub, fit for a swan. Like the
very rich, many designers are hooked by possessions, and
the more they buy at auction, the more they seem to want.
Until, as with Gloria, much ends up, forgotten, in ware-
houses.

She fixed me with her very black, mascaraed eyes, deter-

mined as always, and observed proudly, "You know, John"
—waving her arm gracefully—"everything here I bought
with the money I've earned from my own hard work."

I could see the lights from across the East River twinkling
beyond the balcony railing (the same balcony from which,
in the summer of 1988, her twenty-three-year-old son, Car-
ter, would jump to his death).

Gloria's life has been stalked by tragedy. She lost her
third husband, Wyatt Cooper, the man she really loved,
when he died tragically during heart surgery at New York
Hospital. Cooper had the charming look of a refined Hollywood cowboy and Gloria had been so much in love with
him that one day she impulsively caught a plane for Los
Angeles, searched him out in a motel, and persuaded him
to return to New York and marriage. Women designers are
a determined lot, take it from me. Much stronger than the
men.

Unfortunately, Gloria was to make a string of bad business decisions, selling her name into commercial slavery
for quick money. Then, for a year she was secluded at 10
Gracie Square, convinced that her son had died in a tragic
accident. She was greatly comforted by Nancy Reagan, a
close friend, who often stayed with her. It was to Gloria's
home that Nancy went after she had a partial facelift. Both
women have taken solace in reading the stars.

When I ran into Gloria at The Four Seasons recently, she
was looking great but said she planned to sell her apartment and move to Santa Fe.

Gloria Vanderbilt and Mary McFadden—both products
of what could be called the American aristocracy—daring,
slightly mad, tossed aside convention in their personal lives,
remaining in society while venturing out to do battle in the
savage world of fashion. They were to be followed by other
women of the cloth, including Carolina Herrera, a favorite
of Jackie Onassis; Vicomtesse Jacqueline de Ribes, aristo-
cratic to the tip of her nose; and Krizia (Mariuccia Man-

delli), a designer as ferocious as the animals on her signature sweaters.

But now it was time for male designers to join the parade to high society. First Bill Blass and then Oscar de la Renta struck gold and became part of America's top social scene in the sixties. Both got there with hard work, some creative talent, and lots and lots of charm. It wasn't long before invitations to the de la Renta dinner table or weekends with Blass were readily accepted by tycoons and shakers from all over the world.

Today both Blass and de la Renta are very much part of the Kent, Connecticut, gang, led by Nancy and Henry Kissinger. In fact, the Kissingers were persuaded to settle in Kent by Oscar, who helped them find their house. Weekends, to the Kissingers of Kent, comes a parade of world leaders and their power friends from here and abroad. Towering Nancy, her ever-present cigarette in hand, receives guests in her down-to-earth way and proffers course after course of delicious food (lobsters and steaks from the grill, cheese, pies and cakes), even on the hottest of days.

We were there for lunch once in the fall, and Nancy, who had just ripped out an ancient blueberry patch (the local environmentalists were still screaming in the press), proudly showed off her new garden, blowing a plume of cigarette smoke along the path as we walked. Dr. K. stayed inside, and when we returned, he asked for a fire. But he didn't know where the wood was, so Nancy, John Gutfreund, and I trotted off to the shed, and Nancy K. made the fire—and a good one at that—with a little help from Gutfreund.

Oscar de la Renta leaves his new apartment at Sixty-sixth Street and Park Avenue, slumps into the back of his black Mercedes limousine, and instructs his Dominican driver to proceed to 550 Seventh Avenue—a nondescript mini-skyscraper where American fashion is made but not necessarily created.

Oscar is replaying in his mind's eye last night's *Forbes* magazine anniversary party given by publisher Malcolm Forbes for and with a cast of thousands. Everyone, apparently, was there, from Elizabeth Taylor to the Kissingers (musts for any big-time party), many of them arriving by helicopter on the lawn of the Forbes estate in Far Hills, New Jersey. Forbes is everywhere all over the world these days, and his mania for getting his name in publications, including his own, is legendary.

As the driver nears the office, Oscar tries, unsuccessfully, to push tough, ugly Seventh Avenue out of his mind by thinking about his two thousand orange trees, recently planted in his native land. He anticipates oranges and orange juice stamped "de la Renta" being exported soon. It will be the *chic* orange juice.

Getting out of the yacht-long Mercedes, he slides across the beige leather seat, smelling that smart leather aroma. Down Fashion Avenue the other limousines are lining up, each one owned by a designer. Now Oscar gets in the elevator, and Ralph Lauren and Geoffrey Beene are there, all their thoughts turning to the day ahead. Beene usually doesn't speak to others in the Business, but this morning he condescends to nod a small greeting. He has been chauffeured here in his Mercedes station wagon, still one step above the others.

These are some of America's top designers, all working in the same beehive—Blass will pull up a few minutes later —buzzing around the same honeycomb, where money and more money and multiple underground deals are made in the name of something called "fashion."

A designer's nationality really has nothing to do with ability to create fashion. Fashion is truly international. Still, we are waiting for an American designer to set up shop in Paris, London, or Milan. About the only American to make the Paris scene has been Patrick Kelly, a young black designer from the Deep South who has been embraced by the Chambre Syndicale du Prêt-à-Porter des Couturiers et des Créateurs de Mode. Americans generally have not made the jump across the ocean yet, but I'm convinced they will. Already Ralph Lauren has had big success in London and in Paris, and he is even selling to the Milanese right in the heart of Armani country.

Certainly the look of fashion has long been international. A Bill Blass can be worn in any country in the world. Nevertheless, the look is not always the same from country to country. A designer fights to maintain his individuality and yet knows he cannot go against a fashion look that has been accepted. There are exceptions: Yves Saint Laurent, Emanuel Ungaro, Karl Lagerfeld, Christian Lacroix, and Giorgio Armani are, as we have seen, capable of making the big fashion change that keeps fashion alive.

As fashion becomes even more international in scope, the manufacturing and marketing of it will become even more intense. Ralph Lauren will have the choice of making his clothes everywhere and selling them in many more countries. Already we see young Swiss pedaling their mountain bikes up the Alps in their Ralph Lauren polo shirts. And in Milan there are more Ralph Lauren than Armani polo shirts. American designers are beginning to think on a grander, even more international, scale. Bill Blass isn't going to be happy licensing his clothes just in Japan. As a matter of fact, the American rage to do business with the Japanese has subsided. The distance, the cultural differences, and the Japanese way of doing business have befuddled and frustrated the Americans.

Probably the American designers with the greatest sense of merchandising—Ralph Lauren and Calvin Klein—stand the best chance of expanding into the world's markets.

Unfortunately, as we have seen, American designers are tied up in knots because they have confined themselves to manufacturing in the United States with its Seventh Avenue traditions and union problems. They will have to break out into Europe and the Far East—soon—if they are to survive in the international fashion jungle and not sit by and watch the European designers dominate the high-fashion and luxury markets.

12
LAND OF THE
RISING SOCIETY

Birds are chirping sweetly over my FM radio: recorded bird chirps wake you at the Okura Hotel in Tokyo, where I am in a Japanese-style suite, sleeping on the floor with one leg sprawled across the futon, my toes touching the cool tatami mat. That November morning the sun streams through the shoji screen and the rays fall onto a huge white orchid plant, which I received as a gift. Outside, real birds, tiny sparrows, chirp along with the birds singing on my radio.

I get up on my knees and push myself upright by grasping onto the straw top of my futon, now wobbling under my weight. I'm too tall: I whack my head on the wooden beam at the entrance to the bathroom, which, thank God, has been redone since last time: the Japanese toilet you must squat over has been replaced with a Western one.

"Good morning, Mr. Fairchild"—when you pick up the phone at the Okura you are addressed by name. "How are you today?" asks the harmonious sweet voice of room service, obliging, ready to serve. But ordering breakfast is not all that simple. I want those delicious toasted corn muffins that are on the breakfast menu in the dining room downstairs but not on the room-service menu. I begin: "Please" —not as softly spoken as the little Japanese voice—"I don't understand how you can give me toasted corn muffins downstairs and not up here."

"Please, could you wait a moment, Mr. Fairchild?" Pause, then wonderful sweet music. "Yes, we have the muffins, but do you mind waiting forty minutes?"

I would wait forever just to prove a point.

Ten minutes later, the doorbell rings, and there is a very pretty Japanese girl with pigtail with my breakfast. I slip my long legs under the green lacquer table set with a crisp, clean yellow tablecloth and a silver finger bowl with purple-and-white orchid petals. I move the chair back and the cushion closer in. (My back and all my bones are sore from last night's tough shiatsu massage by a woman who kept smiling every time I let out a scream as she worked me over.) I lift the top off the delicate straw basket, open the starched napkin, and inside are Japanese-style English muffins.

I am by now so obsessed with my project that after breakfast I go to the manager's office, where he takes notes and promises toasted corn muffins for tomorrow.

The next morning the same waitress, all smiles, is at my

door. Napkin in lap, piping hot coffee, butter, cooled by ice in a silver bowl and decorated with a small parsley sprig. Off with the basket: English muffins.

The Japanese corn-muffin system had triumphed. No way could the commands be changed even if that sweet girl on the telephone wanted to please me—as I assume she did. Her Japanese pride would not let her say, "Mr. Fairchild, I cannot get you a corn muffin." That just isn't done in Japan. Now I understand why General MacArthur defeated the Japanese so decisively and why he ruled over their island so effectively: he understood how their minds worked and what they would do to rebuild their country into the world's greatest economic power. We have not learned from our great general: instead of jumping ahead step by step we have just sat by watching the Japanese overwhelm us by working together and working harder.

That same morning I asked Aki Mori, our Japanese publishing partner (*W* and *WWD* are published in Japanese versions) about the eighty-six-year-old Emperor Hirohito, who lay dying at the palace. He told me that the Emperor did not like seeing his own medical bulletins given daily on television. He had asked the household staff to look at a small tree he had planted in the three-hundred-acre garden of the palace. The Emperor, a fine horticulturist, had his priorities. He wanted that little tree, planted with his own hands, to grow in regal splendor, and he knew that some of the Japanese leftists had suggested razing the Imperial Palace and gardens, which are right in the center of downtown Tokyo, to make way for public housing.

Emperor Hirohito's dynasty was restored in 1868 with his grandfather and grandmother, Emperor Meiji and Empress Shoken, who in official portraits done in 1895 closely resembled in dress and composure the British Victorian Royal Family. To this day the Imperial Family of Japan emulates and admires the British Royals. In a way the Japanese Imperial Family is Nouvelle royalty compared to those of Europe and China.

I walked around the Imperial Palace's outer walls, which are surrounded by a moat in which swans float gracefully. All along the route, crowds waited in line to sign the Imperial book to wish the Emperor a speedy recovery. One Communist member of the Diet had signed, saying it was his duty even though it was against party principles. The Japanese press had pitched tents outside the main gate as the death watch went on and on.

Aki Mori (who was educated at Dartmouth College) picked me up at the Hotel Okura with his two beautiful black-eyed daughters, Izumi, six, and Yuki, four years old. We were taking the girls for an outing in the 179-acre Inner Garden of Meiji Jingu shrine dedicated to Japan's first emperor and empress of the restoration.

Yuki took my hand, and kept looking way up at me. She must have thought this giant *gaijin* (foreigner) looked strange even though she herself was half-American. (Her mother, Pamela, is a tall, thin California Caucasian.) We bounded up the stairs into a dressing room filled with racks of white Budo-Gi robes, ranging from large to very small. The girls quickly changed and bounced into a gymnasium like little white jumping beans. Time for Budo, a form of martial arts based on an ancient fighting practice.

Martial arts for little girls? What would the women at Greenwich Country Day think of this room filled with both boys and girls from age four up to the early teens, all in their elegant white Budo-Gis ready to roll themselves all over the floor in perfect formation? This is no competition or combat, but discipline and respect for each other and for their parents. Budo is spiritual: it aims for perfection of a human being both in mind and spirit.

I watched the smiling instructor take my little friend Yuki by the shoulders and throw her to the floor gently, and then reach for the next child and do the same thing. Up Yuki popped, smiling, bowed, and returned to the line with the others. In the corner the older boys stood one by one in front of the instructor; he drew his samurai sword and lunged at each boy, who stepped gracefully aside just in time. Discipline. No noise: three instructors directing seventy-five children. In an outer room mothers and fathers sat cross-legged on the floor, watching. As I paced across the room photographing the scene I felt foolish and very foreign, but no one looked at me.

Outside again, Aki and I started to walk through the woods. I had been impressed and I was praising Budo. Aki smiled with pride. He had been mugged in a New York subway and rarely returned to America now unless he had to. He is a tall, proud Japanese with little obvious left of his American education. When he talked about his own country, he was frank about admitting the Japanese wartime brutality, but kept reminding me: "We had to expand to survive. We are a small island with no natural resources and oil. You Westerners cut us off from our resources, so we fought to survive. At the end we sent our aircraft and warships out to sea with not enough fuel to return." Aki blamed World War II on the generals and admirals and even today, like many Japanese, he has little respect for the military.

We were now deep into the heavy woods and Aki was voicing concern as to whether his daughter would be accepted at a first-class Tokyo school, Keio, where entrance guarantees not only top academic credentials to all universities in Japan but into Japan's powerful élite society.

"Very difficult," Aki was saying, for there were only thirty-eight places for a thousand applications. I told him it was just like in New York—the same need for private schools because public education was so bad, but that I couldn't imagine public education in Japan could be as bad as in New York City. And we started talking about America and its problems.

Aki has small eyes that seem to see everything. Now, after seven years of friendship, he looked closely at me and said, "What is wrong with your country is that you have too much individuality, which leads only to selfishness. In Japan we don't have enough individuality but we are changing. The next generation, my children, will be more independent and less disciplined and then Japan will change. But if we become selfish like you, we are going to have real problems."

It had been six years since I had been to Japan, and I could see real changes. The Japanese like us are mired in materialism and greed. They clamor to get into the stores to devour consumer goods like locusts eating up the wheat fields. Millions of sparkling-clean cars and trucks jam their highways, and long bullet trains like giant multicolored dragons speed through the countryside, where almost every plot of land has a factory producing goods for the world. More than 121 million people living on an island just a bit smaller than California have conquered the rest of the industrial world and now are spreading their business tentacles into the lifeline of other countries, including the United States.

The Mori family had invited me for a weekend by the sea in Atami. We were speeding along the highway in a large shiny Nissan and had passed through the Tokyo outskirts. Lining our route were small shack-like houses, some with broken shutters and rusty bicycles in the front yards, and everywhere large and small billboards. In the middle-class areas everything seems to be in need of paint, and the cars dwarf small houses with their lopsided television antennas.

After two hours we arrived at Villa del Sol, a hotel in Atami, famous as a seaside resort and for its earthquakes.

We were escorted to Japanese suites overlooking the sea.

On a black table sat a huge straw basket of tangerines. Aki's famous mother, Madame Hanae Mori, Japan's most international fashion designer, sat gracefully on the floor, her legs folded under her. Next to her was her other son, Kei Mori, who directs part of their world-wide business, seated similarly. I for my part pushed my long legs under the low table but in seconds had to withdraw them as I felt them cramping. Madame Mori's arms moved like a butterfly's wings as she reached for a tangerine. I, too, took a tangerine and was brutally stripping the skin away, ready to bite into the first section, when I stopped. Madame Mori and Kei were removing the skin so delicately that it fell away like petals from a flower. Leaning against my chair rest, I felt like hiding in shame. On the table my tangerine peel lay ready to be picked up by the New York Sanitation Department, while the Moris' peels were orange flowers to be framed. They both were looking at me, and then and there I sensed the difference between our two cultures. Their tangerine was treated as something precious, even in that moment of being devoured, while mine had no such respect.

I was offered a bath in the public waters of the hot springs, but instead I bathed privately in my Japanese bath, sitting on a little stool, soaping up, rinsing my body with a pan and then climbing into the warm spring waters in my wooden tub. I was thankful that no one could see me looking like a fat Buddha. But after my private bath, I couldn't resist walking down some five hundred steps to the public bath and peeking in. The family bathing hours were just ending and a father was leaving with his young daughter. For a moment I found the idea of a family bath quite charming but then I remembered how my twin son and daughter had disapproved when I stripped before entering our South of France pool. (Thereafter, Jill and I confined ourselves to swimming in the nude when we were alone.)

. . .

There is never litter on the streets of Japan in spite of the millions of people. And with all those people crowded together, there are discipline, orderliness, and little noise.

The rich Japanese (according to *Fortune,* the three richest men in the world are Japanese) ride around in black limousines—usually Mercedes or the big Nissans—and sit high in the back seat, with chauffeurs in well-pressed business suits at the wheel. Taxis are spick and span outside and in, with white cotton seat coverings. Cabdrivers wear white gloves and the cab doors open automatically to receive a passenger.

Late at night the pace changes slightly as the Japanese businessman entertains at a restaurant, always in the company of other men: no women are invited. The formality peels away as the men drink lots of scotch. For that short time over his whisky, the Japanese mechanical reserve evaporates and the businessman behaves as a child—playful and silly.

Japan is a paradise for fashion designers, a thriving market where there seems to be no end to a fashion appetite. The Japanese are fashionable in the sense that they want the latest, and even more they want the great names of fashion, especially those ultimate status symbols, Vuitton and Hermès. Basically, the Tokyo Japanese are better dressed and certainly better groomed than most New Yorkers. I don't know any city in the world that has more mass chic. And the predominant influence is all Western: if you looked only at their clothing you could be on Fifth Avenue, New Bond Street, the Faubourg St. Honoré.

Hanae Mori is the best-known Japanese designer, but except when she does evening dresses or a wedding dress, she is not influenced by traditional Japanese looks. Her silk fabrics are, of course, beautifully Japanese. Her clothes travel throughout the world. She creates in Paris a couture collection worn by quietly chic international customers who want superb workmanship and conservative, almost classical, fashions. She has built a large fashion empire and reigns as the Empress Butterfly (her symbol is the butterfly) of Japanese fashion.

She travels six months of the year all over the globe. She was the first Japanese designer to be decorated by the French government, and when the Japanese prime minister is in Washington, Madame Mori is usually invited to the White House. Her power and prestige in Japan are strong: she is one of the few women in Japan who can sit down with the Imperial Family, and she is accepted not only as a designer but as a businesswoman, which is rare indeed in a society that does not let wives outside their homes in the evening, except on rare occasions like weddings.

The Moris, like the rest of the important Japanese firms, have turned to China, their old enemy, for future business expansion. Hanae Mori's interest is the Chinese market in cashmere, the yarn worth its light weight in gold. In partnership with the Chinese she has built modern sweater-knitting factories, with German and Japanese electronic looms, in Puerto Rico. She has managed to corner the cashmere market, avoid all U.S. import duties, and produce a fine high-fashion sweater at prices lower than the English and Italians.

The Mori success story is somewhat typical of the Japanese firms that rose from the ashes after the war. Madame Mori recalls that during the bombing of Tokyo she was in a shelter reading *Gone With the Wind,* absorbed in that story and oblivious of the horrors aboveground. "We will never let the army take over again," she said to me sternly. She was graduated from Tokyo Woman's Christian University, and with her husband, who had been a Supply Corps officer during the war, started a small tailoring business outside of Tokyo. She has always loved Western style, though deep down she is thoroughly Japanese.

As for the rest of creative Japanese fashion, Rei Kawakubo and Yohji Yamamoto, both of whom had a brief moment in the fashion sun, have spent years trying to hide Japanese women's bodies in dreary black to cover any defects in their figure, though recently Kawakubo has added colors. Her clothes found customers among the intellectual Greenwich Villagers and Upper West Side New Yorkers, until stores dropped Japanese fashions when they became overpriced because of the exchange rate. Kawakubo closed her downtown store and Kansai Yamamoto (another Yamamoto) closed his Madison Avenue boutique. The Japanese discovered that most women, even those with bad bodies, want to show off what they have.

My personal opinion of Japanese fashion is negative, and we will stand by our double page, six years ago, at *WWD*, when we put a large X through Kawakubo and Yamamoto's fashions, calling them "Intellectual Bag Ladies." We can well understand why Japanese women prefer and buy much high fashion from French, Italian, and top American designers.

Another Japanese designer, Issey Miyake, carried Japanese fashion disguise even further with yards and yards of fabrics floating like a circus tent around a woman. Miyake, who is always publishing books about his fashion as an art, in his last collection was inspired by corrugated boxes. Bergdorf Goodman, New York's high-fashion retailer, has a Miyake boutique and claims to be doing well but secretly admits to selling some of Miyake's floating-fabric clothes to men. Figure that one out if you care to.

Another Japanese designer, Kenzo, fled Japan and set up shop in Paris, where in the sixties he was considered influential and even for a brief moment inspired couturiers like the mighty Saint Laurent. But then, alas, his clothes were considered too avant-garde, and so to make money (and he did) he tamed his fashions and now sells them in his Madison Avenue boutique. The fashion world no longer looks to him for inspiration, and for the most part his clothes are Westernized—except for a few exotic touches from the Orient.

America—especially the California life style—is part of Japanese life today. America has infiltrated Japanese culture and living to almost frightening dimensions. Blue jeans, music, fast food, baseball, basketball, golf, and fashion—all of it is in Japan; even English-language road signs and American advertisements. Japanese are buying up Hawaii, vacationing there, and sending their top talent to America to learn.

Yet we as Americans have failed to capitalize on the Americanization of Japan. Instead of sending them Made in USA, they are sending us Made in Japan. Why?

The American Embassy will tell you that Americans are still not making a big enough effort to enter the Japanese market. In the words of former ambassador Mike Mansfield, who was venerated by the Japanese almost as much as was MacArthur: "The Pacific basin is where business is happening now and for the future, and Americans will have to be there." But we had better get to work there fast. The French and Italians are already making a big push to the Far East—including Korea, which is already a big competitor of Japan's.

With all their economic power and world travel, there still remains among many élite Japanese a lack of sophistication in the Western sense. But then why should the Japanese want to become Westernized? When they do take on Western airs it does not quite work. When the Japanese go

"Western" in interior decoration, the outcome is usually hideous.

In service and presentation and sometimes even in food, their Western-food restaurants are equal to the best European and American ones, but there is always that little oddity. Nevertheless, their one mission is to please their customers.

There I was sitting in the Tour d'Argent, Tokyo, one of the most expensive restaurants in the world. The glasses were glistening in the candle-lit room, with shadows playing on the Louis XVI oak *boiserie* that had been shipped over panel by panel from France. The French headwaiter in tails was shorter than the rest of the Japanese restaurant staff, and he was gliding across the floor effortlessly as if on a skateboard pulled by a string. As he passed an empty table he touched each chair delicately, making sure it was in exactly the right place. We could hear the swish of his tails as he came closer and bent to receive our commands. He quietly informed us that every duck served at the Tour d'Argent was numbered and that when the Emperor had visited Tokyo in 1921 the number on his duck was 53,211—or was it 53,212? Somehow, the Emperor's duck number seemed unimportant when we knew the man himself lay dying right around the corner, but our Japanese hosts seemed interested.

Japanese society revolves around the Japanese Imperial Family, who until recently rarely left their enclosed palace grounds. But with Akihito on the throne, a man who is said to be strongly influenced by his wife Michiko (a commoner), there is the feeling of changes to come. Akihito's younger brother, Prince Hitachi, educated at Oxford, is seen abroad and is as popular with the Japanese public as Prince Charles is in England.

The most powerful families in Japan are ten in number. These Big Ten have ties to politicians (ex-premiers are very powerful) and to the Imperial Household. They are not necessarily the richest but they are the most respected in a tightly knit society. These families are linked together into a giant chain that pulls in one direction for Japan. Their hard work and manpower, mobilized in a grand effort, have put Japan over the top. How long the new generation will work at their back-breaking pace is the big question now.

Japan has its Nouvelle Society as well, in the person of Yoshiaki Tsutsumi, whom the Japanese call the Donald Trump of Japan—but he is much richer than Trump. Tsutsumi is, according to *Fortune*, the third-richest man in the world. He is owner of a conglomerate that includes railways, the Prince hotel chain, golf courses, clubs, and a baseball team, the Seibu Lions. He is also heavily into real estate and construction. Perhaps one day Donald Trump and he will compare notes.

To have a glimpse of the inner world of Japanese wealth is extremely difficult because the wealthy do not invite anyone except relatives and a few friends into their homes. And, as we have seen, Japanese wives rarely make public appearances, and if they do are severely criticized.

The one home I have seen inside is that of the Moris. A small white-tiled house built right in the middle of Tokyo and designed by the famous architect, Kenzo Tange, it is an ultramodern box outside but inside comfortable and quietly decorated by English designer David Hicks. I stepped out of a Nissan into a courtyard with a delicate and beautiful bamboo garden in the middle, the leaves rustling and the stalks bending like Japanese dancers in the light breeze. Two maids in black uniform with white aprons led me inside to a living room that could have been one in Paris or New York. Dom Pérignon in Baccarat stem glasses was served by the manservant in a smartly tailored black jacket and gray trousers. The dinner, half French, half Japanese, and all fantastic, was cooked by a Japanese chef who trained in Paris.

After dinner, because we had raved, the chef appeared

graciously in his toque and took a bow, in part for the small, thinly sliced Japanese sweet potatoes, and in part for a classical dinner that was better in presentation and quality than any I have had in France or the United States. Afterward we went upstairs to an ultramodern hideaway: one side of the room was a sleek kitchen with a large bar table and stools. That is where the family meet for breakfast, especially on Sundays, in their American blue jeans. As the evening moved on, Kei Mori pulled out the television set, and we saw ourselves on video eating the dinner of minutes before. Right then and there I decided to go on a diet.

But for an official evening it is a different story.

The black limousines with bodyguards and walkie-talkies are drawn up outside Kitcho, Japan's finest and most exclusive restaurant, hidden away in a dark alley in the middle of Tokyo. Only Japan's élite and a few foreign guests can dine there, and as they do the restaurant keeps a record of their menus so that no one ever has the same dish again. Entering, we take off our shoes, put on soft slippers, shuffle to an elevator, and then into a brightly lit room, where the guests bow to each other, the women servers bow to you and with a gentle motion of an outstretched arm guide you to your seat on the floor. Then the struggle to get my long legs comfortably under the table begins. Even saki and beer don't relieve the aches and pains of sitting on the floor.

The night I was there I was the guest of the Mori family —Hanae, Aki, and Kei. We were having dinner with old friends, our American Ambassador, Mike Mansfield, and his wife, Maureen, one of my favorite women. It was the night the Mansfields told us they were ending their tour of duty in Japan.

"Mr. Ambassador," Aki Mori asked, "have you ever met Emperor Hirohito and what did you say to him?" Mansfield said that he had met the Emperor at official receptions and when he escorted American Presidents to the palace. He recalled that Gerald Ford couldn't find a morning suit to fit him, but he went to the palace anyway with his trousers much too short: it didn't bother him or the Emperor. But Mansfield never told us anything the Emperor said, though he described the Emperor's first visit to the American Embassy after the defeat of Japan. The Emperor left his household staff in the small library and walked alone the length of the long embassy salon to General MacArthur, who was behind his desk in his uniform but with an open shirt. The Emperor, top hat in hand, bowed. Mansfield added that it was very good that the Emperor had been kept on, for he provided a unifying force at a critical time. As he talked, Mansfield was cooking his prawns on a burning stone grill or sipping saki served gracefully to him by a woman on her knees. A saki cup, it seems, must always be kept filled. Out of the corner of my eye I saw the soup arrive. I took off the top of my bowl: inside there was a small piece of snapping turtle in the brownish broth.

Maureen, who had never been able to master the use of chopsticks, was eating sushi—raw tuna and sea bream—with a knife and fork. She told us many American designers, including Blass and Geoffrey Beene and Oscar de la Renta, had passed through Tokyo. "They all are coming here and doing great business," said Hanae Mori. I thought to myself there was really no escaping designers: they are going everywhere in the world. And now the French and Italians were pushing on to Korea and Taiwan.

We were about to eat grilled crab when the subject of Ferdinand and Imelda Marcos came up. Maureen remembered her last visit to the Philippines, when the Marcoses were still in power. The Mansfields entered a throne room where Ferdinand sat on his throne "way above us, just staring down at us as if he didn't know who we were. And we were old friends."

We were eating quail as Maureen fascinated us with early stories of Imelda Marcos and the way she had lost her enthusiasm and turned hard.

Finally—the meal seemed to go on forever—we were having vegetables: buckwheat nut and yam nut. Next course, Kobe beef (probably the most tender in the world), which we had cooked on our own charcoal grill. Next, steamed rice and pickles. And, at long last, dessert: melon and persimmon followed by chestnut cake and that soothing medicinal green tea.

As we walked out, Ambassador Mansfield warmly saluted with a wave, then bowed slightly to the Mori family, and said, "Well, you Japanese have come so far. You are big boys now and ready to shoulder the responsibility."

As I rode back to the hotel alone through the streets of Tokyo I looked up. Everywhere lights flashing in all colors filled the sky with advertisements: buy this, buy that. I hoped Mike Mansfield was right about the Japanese shouldering international responsibility.

The next morning Aki Mori met me downstairs, and I couldn't resist asking him: "How much was the dinner last night at Kitcho?" He told me: "Five hundred dollars per person. And that menu was simplified for foreigners like you."

Afterward, I realized why I had asked such a rude question. I needed to confirm to myself what I already knew: The Japanese now have the power and the money.

13
AWAY FROM IT ALL

I'll admit it. I want to go on forever chasing after Chic Savages. I regret none of the experiences I've lived through. But I need to escape my Savage world from time to time.

Klosters, Switzerland, is my real escape. But is it an escape living fifteen hundred meters up in the Alps? Or is this village life more real and wonderful than the New York-Paris-London-Milan life down below?

Outside my window the grass is green and filled with acres of Queen Anne's lace, some white, some pink.

We rise early in the morning to catch the sun rising over the Pischahorn. Soon the rays will flood the doll house in which we live, Châlet Bianchina. Quite a pastoral contrast to the party that the Savages are still talking about—a party that took place just as we got here this August of 1988. It was a $2 million affair given in Villefranche on the Côte d'Azur by Lily, wife of Edmond J. Safra, one of the world's richest bankers, to celebrate Edmond's birthday and the final redecorating of La Leopolda, a house built by Belgium's King Leopold II for his mistress, and later owned by the Agnellis. No expense was spared for this Nouvelle evening—flowers from Holland, Sergio Mendes and his entire orchestra flown in from California, a hurricane-proof Pompeii-style tent, food by Roger Verge of Moulin de Mougins (*soupe de poisson, feuilleté aux asperges,* and *saumon aux truffes*), a French SWAT squad—half a man per guest—to protect the glorious three hundred who were arriving, some of them by boat. Valentino's new $20 million yacht, *TM Blue,* was ready in time for the party (after Valentino threatened a lawsuit) and she dieseled into the Villefranche harbor with Mikhail Baryshnikov on board. But the Niarchos mega-yacht *Atlantis II* with its helicopter stole the show.

Everyone who saw Valentino's yacht wanted to know where he got so much money. Lagerfeld, Ungaro, and many other designers kept asking me, "How can Valentino sell so many dresses?" But when we in turn questioned Giancarlo Giammetti, Valentino's brilliant partner and business brains, he was irate: "Why don't you worry more about our dresses and less about our social and private life?" And then he added, "We last year did $250 million of business with GFT [Italy's biggest top-quality fashion manufacturer]. I want to be treated as a serious businessman. Just stop all the nonsense." I could answer only: "No question, you are a great businessman and Valentino is one of the top-selling designers in the world, but don't forget his life style fascinates everyone, even the people attending the Safra ball." We had heard that Safra was one of Valentino's bankers.

Many of the characters racing about in this book were at the Safra party: Barbara Walters, Karl Lagerfeld, Betsy Bloomingdale, the Taubmans (Judy Taubman was said to look the best of all the ladies, in a black mousseline Dior), the Grimaldis (Prince Rainier and Princess Caroline, who insisted that all the other guests be in place before their entrance), the Rohatyns, the David-Weills, the Wyatts (Lynn Wyatt is a real Texan, the only person I know who has ordered Vuitton luggage in lizard skin), the Livanoses, Marcie-Rivières.

The last word in high etiquette came from Susan Gutfreund (whose husband had flown all night from New York to reach the party). I quote from Dennis Thim's report (written after he was chased from covering the event by the French SWAT on their roaring motorcycles). Madame Gutfreund's final words were: "With the opening of a palace like this, the home and the hostess should be the stars. I wanted to dress to disappear like a rat in the woodwork." And what did she wear for that purpose? A white mousseline Chanel. (Most of the clothes at the party came from Valentino, Dior, and Chanel.) The Safra event itself (followed by a second ball with a B list of mostly bankers and business friends) marked the culmination of the Safras' meteoric rise to social power: they have taken over the Riviera, Southampton, New York, the Metropolitan Opera, Geneva —all in a space of five years. What's next? The headline about the party on our full page in *WWD* read: "The Gilded Lily." It should have read: "Gilding the Lily."

So while the glories of Nouvelle Society and the ultimate in conspicuous consumption plays out in the South of France, we are in Klosters, watching the sun coming over the mountain.

The sun is warm now. I open the windows. Roderick is

spread out, basking with his head between his paws. Outside, a farmer walks through his fields and looks carefully at the hay to see whether he should cut his second crop. What a carpet of flowers—yellow anemones, dark blue gentians, yellow cowslips, wild crimson orchids, blue forget-me-nots—to be eaten by the cows. Their bells echo throughout the valley.

On my breakfast tray, pink iris and blue forget-me-nots accompany freshly baked oat bread from the village and homemade jam from blueberries picked in the mountains. (The amount of blueberries or mushrooms picked is carefully watched by the Klosters police, who ride through the mountain passes in small white cars with orange markings.) The pale red geraniums were watered last night and now trail out of their windowboxes. Our Papa Meilland roses are finally growing and getting new buds: we have stopped the deer from climbing the stairs to eat the buds by placing our car in their path.

The village of Klosters (population under four thousand off season) is reached by a toy train that winds its way up the valley from Zürich. We know the train is coming from the sound of its high-pitched whistle, and at night as we look out our bedroom window, the cars curve around the mountains like a diamond necklace shining bright and then fading away into the pine trees.

In the summer we walk in the mountains for hours until we are exhausted. Below us is the roaring Landquart River, its banks lined with big buttercups, Queen Anne's lace, purple thistles, wild frayed carnations, wild gladioli, and wild strawberries and blueberries. Still further up the valley are yellow foxglove, blue lupines, Turk's cap, and, as we climb, alpine rhododendron and the alpine rose. No one really needs a private garden in Klosters. God has given us his.

Come winter there are the moments when the snow piles up so high around Châlet Bianchina that we have to strain to see over the drifts in front of the French doors. After a big snowfall the valley reverberates with the sound of cannons fired into the mountains by the avalanche patrols to bring down the snow. A loud boom and then a pause and from our balcony I can see a man raising his binoculars in the direction of the cannon fire. Then through my own binoculars I see another shell hit a mound of snow, and black smoke rises. The snow doesn't move. There is another and another shot before there comes that big whoom-roar. It is as if we are under a wave in the sea—a giant tidal wave—as the snow billows up to the sky, then starts coming toward the Châlet Bianchina. The policeman who has blocked the path and road to our house with a flashing sign reading AVALANCHE DANGER stands calmly by. We wonder each time if we should run to our bomb shelter. (Every Swiss home by law is equipped with a shelter; we have turned ours into a wine cellar.) Or should we just get out?

In March of 1988 I watched a policeman through my binoculars as he calmly talked into his walkie-talkie to the artillery in the woods. Finally, I put on my boots and bundled up, though the sun was out and melting the snow already—hot sun dangerously loosens the snow—and with snow up to my waist I took off down the path. The policeman saw me coming but didn't stop me from entering right into the avalanche zone. (I would be able to take the garbage out that night by sled. It is fun racing down the mountain on a small old-fashioned wooden sled clutching a plastic bag.) He told me that the avalanche stopped just short of the main road to the Alpenrösli, a small restaurant above our châlet. The road was still open. British and Swiss security had been up there the day before to check the restaurant for the dinner to be given that night by Prince Charles for his friends and the rest of the royal party. It was a dinner that would never take place. For that afternoon Prince Charles, who had been coming to Klosters for many

years, was skiing with his mountain guide, and with friends
from Klosters, Mr. and Mrs. Charles Palmer-Tomkinson
and Major Hugh Lindsay. They were skiing at their own risk
on a closed run, and just as they were about to cross on the
Haglamatta the mountain gave way and caught Major Lindsay and Mrs. Palmer-Tomkinson, hurling them onto the
boulders. Lindsay was crushed to death, and both of Pattie
Palmer-Tomkinson's legs were broken in many places. It
would be more than six months before she walked out of
the Davos Hospital, and even then she was on crutches.
While she was recovering, Prince Charles made secret trips
to Davos to see her, driving himself up from Kloten airport.
The tragic accident rocked our little village.

Klosterites have a great sense of people, not for who they
are or what they do, but for what they are like. The locals
here respect Prince Charles as a fine, sensitive gentleman
and very much a civilized man. And Klosters is close to
Charles's heart. To his wedding and to most of the pre-
wedding parties he invited his Klosters friends: Ruth Guler,
owner of the Hotel Wynegg and mother superior to all the
English; Jörg and Vreni Egger, the local doctor and his wife;
Hans Hartmann, who sells the Prince and the royal party
their skiing equipment; and his Klosters bodyguard, policeman Stefan Cadruvi.

When visiting Mrs. Palmer-Tomkinson in the hospital
Prince Charles stayed in a simple but beautiful small room
at the Hotel Walserhof, and took his meals there with the
rest of the guests in what is one of the best restaurants in
Switzerland. During the day he set his easel up on the Walserhof balcony and painted.

Privacy is guaranteed in Klosters, even for Greta Garbo,
who has spent her summers here for more than twenty
years. In the beginning she lived in a small apartment,
where she did her own health-food cooking, but as she
reached her eighties she moved into the Pardenn Hotel,

where just this afternoon we saw her taking her five-o'clock walk, not striding quickly as she used to, but aided by a friend. Her face is still that great face, now partly covered by straight gray hair; on her head she was wearing a straw stovepipe hat. Sometimes she ventures down to the village for luncheon and orders a vodka martini at the Chesa Grischuna, a charming inn with local dishes and sophisticated cuisine.

Our author friend Irwin Shaw had a home in Klosters for more than twenty-five years. He loved to ski, and he is still remembered here for the annual "Irwin Shaw race" he set up. I was with Irwin the last time he skied. The snow was soft and treacherous and, because of our weight, we both kept sinking in deeper and deeper. The further in we went, the more we laughed. But when after three hours of fighting Wolfgang—a proper name for a wicked and dangerous run —we made it down, we drank lots of *Aigle,* Irwin's favorite white wine.

But with all the celebrities our village has known, to me the most important people are the locals, who, when they know you, make you feel like part of the life here. When we go out early in the morning with our straw shopping basket, we stop by to see Doris and Hans Guler, who own and run the Chesa Grischuna: she is in her late seventies and he is eighty. If they don't see us at the restaurant for a while, they will call and ask us when we are coming. It was at the Chesa that we gave a luncheon for the great fabric designer Gustav Zumsteg and Claudia Mantegazzi, who had motored up in Gustav's pale blue chauffeur-driven Bentley, with Claudia wearing a large blue enamel and diamond Schlumberger ring (a gift from Gustav, who had inherited it from his mother). There we were at the Chesa—just the four of us—eating those wonderful mountain mushrooms gathered by Claude the headwaiter, when Gustav beckoned to his chauffeur across the room. The chauffeur brought a large tan leather suitcase to our table. It stayed there on the banquette next to Claudia as we had the poached turbot, which had arrived fresh that morning, followed by local raspberries in the Chesa's ice cream. It wasn't until coffee came and Gustav lit up a cigar that he gave another signal and Claudia opened the bag and displayed all the outstanding fabrics we had just seen in the Paris collections. He unfurled a solid gold lamé, which Saint Laurent had used for a jacket and with great gusto draped it around Jill. Then out of the suitcase came double-faced satins in black and bright colors from purple to yellow to red, and it was as though Gustav were a painter about to splash his paints onto the canvas. There hadn't been such flamboyance at the Chesa for a long time. We watched, fascinated, as he stretched and stroked his double-faced satins and explained that there were more than four hundred threads in one piece, and that only six looms operated by old women in Lyons could weave such "a splendor."

The fabrics were so magnificent that I asked him: "When will Oscar de la Renta and Bill Blass have these satins?" He took a long puff on his cigar and said, "Never. There is a limited production." I thought to myself the American designers would have to settle for a lesser quality. And then, rather morosely, as Claudia began repacking the suitcase, Gustav added, "I really don't know how long we will be able to create fabrics like this. The hands to weave on these special looms will not exist. Sad."

As Gustav and Claudia sped back through the village in their blue Bentley, we started up the hill to Châlet Bianchina. Just as we entered our dirt road, walled in on each side with old stones, a small doe jumped over the wall in front of us. Behind her was another deer that just couldn't get over the wall. He looked at us and then ran off into the green field, sometimes completely covered by the high Queen Anne's lace. Further up the steep hill we came upon

Emanuel Ungaro, the dynamic Paris designer, climbing hand in hand with Laura Fanfani, her long, bushy hair tied down with a pink bow. They looked like any young couple out for a walk, except that her brown eyes never left Ungaro. We asked them up to the house and they puffed up the hill, followed by Roderick, who took a great fancy to Laura.

"Just a glass of water, that's all we want," Emanuel told me. Laura brushed gently up against him, like a pussycat, as he sat on the couch drinking Klosters water, which flows down to us from the mountain just above the châlet.

It seems they had decided to come over to Klosters for ten days from Saint Moritz, where they had rented film producer Marina Cicogna's house. Years ago, Klosters had been Ungaro's village. He had built one of the handsomest châlets in the village. But, alas, after he and Sonya Knapp had created their home, and she had helped him establish his business, they had had a falling out. Emanuel and Laura left us as quickly as they had come, tramping across the open field through the wild flowers in the direction of his old home. As they disappeared over the hill, dark clouds were forming all around and there was thunder followed by rain. We knew the field would be even greener the next day with a new growth of wild flowers. As Emanuel had said in our living room, "There is such peace here—and the smell of the air—wonderful."

Because of Jill we have become friendly with Jürg Stahel, the forester or, as Jill called him, "the guardian of the forest." He is responsible for the life of more than half a million trees in our rugged valley. And to quote from Jill's interview with him in W, Stahel is confronted each day with the decision of which tree is to live or die. It was Jill and Jürg who brought trees into my life, taught me that each tree has its own personality. The forests are sacred in Switzerland. Jürg had to have an engineering degree and then study for five years before becoming a forester. As he explains, "We as foresters have to deal with the strength and will of nature. We must learn to live with nature. Otherwise man is doomed. Technology is out of control and everything is so fast. We have to reach an equilibrium between technology and nature if we are to survive. There is no turning back. No one wants to make a sacrifice, and here is the danger: that life will end in a catastrophe—that is the issue now."

Then Jürg, who looks like a Jesuit and speaks like a poet, says, "You see trees live inside each one of us. They have a soul which communicates. When I am sad or happy, their presence stabilizes things."

Along with our châlet in Klosters, we have a secret paradise I have already shared with you, Mas Daumas, our seventeenth-century farmhouse in Gordes, France. About the only factor the two places have in common is that they are away from all that we are used to—sometimes so far away that we feel really cut off until the telephone rings. Mas Daumas, too, overlooks a range of mountains, the Lubéron, but they would never be called mountains by the Swiss.

To get to Mas Daumas, we are obliged to take Air Inter, the French domestic airline, which seems always to be on strike—for a day, a week, or a month. Or there is the TGV from Paris, a train that floats like a magic carpet in just four hours from Paris to Avignon.

Today we landed at Marignan, a fine airport outside Marseilles, and now, speeding along the Autoroute du Soleil, we can smell, even over the fumes of the highway, the yellow broom swaying to the winds of the mistral. On each side of the highway are orchards—pear, peach, cherry, apricot—protected from the high winds by those elegant poplars.

The approach to our farm passes through Cavaillon, a city

known as the fruit and vegetable basket, for it provides the best in produce for all of France. Just price a Cavaillon melon in Paris or New York, and you know those Cavaillonese have got to be rich.

Out of Cavaillon into the open country, there are vineyards and cherry orchards on both sides of the road. The Lubéron Mountains look like giant pincushions over the plain. In front of us the perched village of Gordes is almost lost in the sky as it stands out alone.

A left turn off the main road, a right up a potholed road, which gives way to dirt and stones, a right again onto an even narrower road overrun with scrub, white oaks and pines, and we can smell rosemary, thyme, savory. Roderick starts to bark. Does he recognize the road or smell the herbs? Our unpaved road is made only for Jeeps, which can bounce along, in and out of the potholes and over the large rocks.

No one can find their way to our house, no matter how many times they have been here. Not even the French security guards assigned to Henry and Nancy Kissinger could get them to dinner at Mas Daumas. We met the Kissingers and their entourage at the bottom of the hill and drove them through the undergrowth to our house. The security guards took one look and decided it was safe enough to leave the Kissingers with their own bodyguard at least for dinner. So the French security left, but then couldn't find their way back after dinner.

We are just passing our small seventeenth-century "ruin" now restored into a guest house with a small living room and kitchen carved out of a borie (piles of stone making a cavelike room dating back thousands of years and believed to have been used for animals), and a studio looking out onto a courtyard shaded by an old olive tree. I can hear the trickle of water coming from the fountain, which runs softly into a water basin filled with water lilies and papyrus.

We are there. We walk up the stairs through the small woods and past our stone statue of a dog, which looks so real other dogs bark, and before us is our garden: lavender, rosemary, sage, santolina, box, all the shades of gray and green. Up the old walls in the outer courtyard are roses, some as big as small cabbages, and some, the yellow mermaid, tiny. Roses have climbed up the oak tree outside our bedroom window. In the middle of the small garden, reigning supreme, is a three-hundred-year-old olive tree. We go up a tiny step and past two straight holly trees guarding the entrance to our box garden, which overlooks the Apt Valley with the Lubéron Mountains enclosing us in our own private world.

Greeting us is Laurance, an Olympic housekeeper, guardian of the Mas Daumas, and a cook to top any chef we know. Laurance is a perky, independent twenty-seven-year-old, who can repair anything, from the furnace to the electric wiring, and who maintains the pool and sees to it that the gardener does his job. About the only problem that can put her out of sorts is bugs. She doesn't like any of them, and neither do we. Mas Daumas has its families of creepy, crawly creatures, including spiders that spin webs over the doorways, scorpions that get into shoes left out overnight and under pillows when the beds are empty. Then we have deadly *frelons* that nest in the walls; the stings of these wasps can be lethal. And when they built their castle in the attic, it took the local fire brigade in masks and boots to gas them out.

Once Pat Buckley was taking a bath at Mas Daumas when she heard a munching noise in the cupboard under the bathroom sink. She got out of the tub and opened the cupboard door to find large mice (a special French variety) nesting. Geraldine Stutz, who likes her sleep more than most people, was dozing away in the brass bed under a canopy of chintz lilacs, while the rest of us who had finished

breakfast under the grape arbor hours before were enjoying the early-morning sun. Suddenly we heard a horrible
scream from Stutz's bedroom. A giant grasshopper had
jumped right under her nightie into her bosom. It was indeed the biggest grasshopper we had ever seen.

We have other exotic creatures, like wild boars, running
through our garden, and on hot days they lounge at the pool.
Farmers from nearby villages come to us looking for their
wild sheep, which often run loose on the plateau. Otherwise, we don't see many locals except for our next-door
neighbor, Paul Bertrand, who helped us set the stories of
murder and ghosts at Mas Daumas to rest.

It all started when a farmer who was delivering us some
firewood said, "Why didn't you tell me this was your house
where that famous murder took place?" Jill and Jillie
turned pale, for they are both afraid of ghosts. At that time
Jillie, who was sleeping in the blue bedroom, had started
having terrible nightmares about knives, blood, and lop-
ping-off of heads. She had rarely had bad dreams before.
And so after the farmer called ours the house of the murder, we started talking about how spooky Provence can be
at night. And Jill kept pointing out that on our long walks
Roderick stopped and put his tail between his legs and just
stood staring at one special spot. So we began to accept the
fact that our dream house was haunted.

Then when Paul Bertrand came over for drinks one night,
we asked him about it, and he put his glass down and
roared with laughter. "Of course, it's true. There was a
murder in which a son killed his drunken father with a
crowbar—but that happened in my house. I still have the
murder weapon."

In our first year at Mas Daumas, we were often without
lights at night. Our electric panel sat on a board in a small
forest of oaks. In the middle of a dinner we would rush out
to the panel and tinker with the switches to restore the

lights. Then we discovered that we did not have enough voltage to run Mas Daumas, which depends on electricity for everything, including the heating and the pumps for our own well. Water is a precious commodity on the plateau, and so we have built two cisterns to store our supply. That first year we were here, I told our guests that water for the plants took priority over their baths.

We used to stand for hours holding the hose over each plant. Then we solved our watering problem by installing the drip system invented by the Israelis, which turned their country green. "Goutte à goutte," as the French call the system, keeps our garden blooming gloriously, and we even have raspberries. At night after enjoying a leisurely bath— we now have enough water—I stroll out into our garden and turn on the red valve and hear the water gushing gently onto each plant.

In the early evening light, Mas Daumas has a soft glow of sandy beige and just a touch of red. As we sit under the grape arbor, which runs the whole length of the house, and look out over the Lubéron, the mountains seem to be coming closer. I can see the cedar forest on top of the mountains, and right in front of me our pine forest sways as the light so famous in Provence plays on the trees in many shades of green. Clouds puffing all the way up to heaven look like enormous lions sitting there in outer space. A squadron of swifts dives close to the arbor and then swoops down over the pool way below.

Jill sits next to me in her green-and-white-flower-printed Ungaro with a white cashmere shawl draped over her shoulders. On her feet are those little red strap shoes that somehow can walk across the graveled terrace. We kiss and hold hands for a moment, knowing without saying how lucky we are to be there together. Then Laurance's sister, Marianne, brings the drinks tray, and we have the local cassis, white wine, and Perrier. On the tray are local olives (in the market that morning we counted at least twenty different varieties), almonds, tiny slices of Gruyère, and pieces of salami. We sip our red cassis out of those wonderful blue-green sea-bubble glasses from Biot.

"Madame, le dîner est servi," Marianne says in her singsong Provençal accent. The table covered in a pale blue Indian seersucker cloth sits at one end of the arbor. On white plates from Moustiers Marianne has placed orange Cavaillon melons still in their striped green rinds, our local bread, and a young, very light, simple red Bordeaux, just slightly chilled. Our main course is thin pasta with two sauces—tomato and pesto (without pine nuts), made with our own olive oil and basil from the garden. A simple lettuce salad, goat cheese from nearby, and then Laurance's kiwi and raspberry sherbet with *tuiles* (thin, lacy almond cookies) which come from a bakery in Cabrières that specializes in this irresistible delight. After dinner we take our vervain tea, made from leaves just plucked from the kitchen garden minutes ago.

It is still so light we do not want to go to bed. We sit there and talk every night until the sky above is filled with millions of stars.

But with all this natural beauty surrounding us, we still need to be with people, and so entertaining outside—at luncheon or dinner—is just a natural event. Lunch starts at one, with innocent drinks—wine, Campari, cassis and Perrier—and then, if there are many people, ten or twelve, we move out of the courtyard to the large table under the fig and oak trees. We don't finish until around four and we talk and talk. There is something about being outside under those trees that just makes for wonderful, stimulating conversation. Perhaps it is because no matter who is there they are relaxed. And really no one in Provence seems to care about success, money, and power; they care more about what they can give to others in friendship or stimulation. Not necessarily intellectual either. I am the last person who could be labeled a "double dome," as they used to call an intellectual. I had a hard enough time graduating from Princeton in the days when it was rather easy.

Our favorite evenings at Mas Daumas are usually spent with Sir Stephen Spender, the English poet, with a face straight off an old Grecian coin, and his wife, Natasha, as charming as the tiny straw hat and English garden-print dress she sometimes wears. Tonight they have brought the Baileys. John Bailey is a professor of English at Oxford, and Iris Murdoch, his wife, the great novelist, now says seriously as she looks out over the valley to the Lubéron: "How beautiful—just so beautiful your garden and the house. Why, you could put a string quartet out on that rock in the distance and they could play into the night." We had never thought of it, but Iris was right: that cliff extending out over the valley would be the perfect place for a quartet. After dinner, the Baileys and the Spenders cram into their little car and start down the driveway and stop just in front of the ruin. Stephen gets out of the car and suggests it will be better if I drive the Baileys to the main road as the Spender car is scraping bottom. Iris and John jump into the back seat of our Peugeot station wagon and we are off down the winding road. As we stop, Professor Bailey asks to speak to me privately. "John, I must tell you and I hope you don't mind but on the left side of your car there is a squeak. I thought you should know." I just love this story and have told it over and over again.

One of our largest dinner parties at Mas Daumas was given in honor of Florette and Jacques-Henri Lartigue, the late, great photographer, who when he was close to ninety was one of the most elegant gentlemen we ever knew. He was the only French photographer to have his pictures in a permanent exhibit at the Grand Palais—all of them with his signature and his drawing of the sun and its rays. He once told us he was rarely in a bad mood and if he was, "I always feel better when I go for a long walk." I remember that at our party, held inside because it was chilly, Jill went out of the room for a moment and when she returned Lartigue stood up, absolutely straight. The rest of the men in the room followed suit.

Rory Cameron, Prince of Provence, as we all called him, was the second one to stand up so elegantly. Rory helped Jill fix the interior of Mas Daumas. He also laid out the bones of our garden.

The first time we went to luncheon at Les Quatre Sources, Rory's house, over the hill and valley from us, we felt immediately that we had found a marvelous friend, and we were to find out that each time we were in his presence we learned something new, something exciting. There we were outside on his terrace overlooking the village of Ménerbes and being served by a butler in a white jacket. Yet after the first course Rory took his plate off the table and let his four quite ferocious dogs (mixed breeds) approach and lick the leftovers. The other guests looked at the prince and, reluctantly, gave their Picasso plates—original Picassos—to the dogs, who licked them dry.

Rory Cameron had about the best eye of anyone we have known. When he was talking to the painter about the color in our living room, he showed him the back side of an olive leaf. When we were in Nantucket he would walk into an antique shop and immediately spot the most interesting objects and wiggle his finger, which meant, Buy it, John.

As the summers passed we sailed with Rory on Anne Cox Chambers's yacht, and he was the tour guide. He gathered us all in a Greek amphitheater, and Stephen Spender, who had just that morning learned he was to be knighted (we heard the news over the ship's radio), recited parts of a Greek play as we all looked on.

On one Fourth of July Anne Chambers invited French, Americans, and, yes, the English to a dinner to celebrate

Independence Day. Anne recited her own poem for the day from a tiny balcony overlooking one of the prettiest gardens in the area.

We live among garden lovers, and some are so serious that when they come to our house, I feel rather ignorant when they ask me the Latin name for a plant. One of the most serious plant lovers of the group is the Baroness de Waldner, known to us as Lulu. She is a handsome woman, strong-looking and strong in character. When we first moved into Mas Daumas she gave us a special vine with large, rather ugly diamond-shaped leaves. Lulu planted it herself next to a wall ("That's the only place") and almost overnight Lulu's plant moved up the wall. By the next summer it had taken over not only our roses but the wall itself, and if we had let it, that clinging vine would have pulled the stones out and the wall would have crumbled.

Years later Lulu was coming over for a visit. I went to pick her up at the Les Beaumettes parking lot. She was sitting on the wall with her straw basket. Usually Lulu carried a flower from her garden in a vial of water, but this time, because it was getting close to winter, she had attached to her basket a Davy Crockett tail of dyed purple fur. On the way to the house, I had to tell her that her tenacious vine had been removed: I knew she would see that it was gone. "Of course. That's right. You had to take it away," she consoled me. I didn't dare ask her why she gave it to us in the first place. Lulu's plant sprouted again this year—indestructible.

One day last summer we were winding down the mountainous road into the gorge overlooking the twelfth-century Abbaye de Sénanque. The abbey and its acres and acres of lavender fields planted in perfect rows is to me one of the most inspiring and beautiful sights I have ever seen.

We started to climb past the abbey, past that lavender field, which seems to extend to the heavens, to take a sharp turn down a rocky road to the house of Père Grégoire, a Cistercian monk who has become a very special friend. We were bringing him eggs, cookies, some fresh strawberry jam Jill had made, and tea. We stopped in his field and saw an acanthus growing from seeds he had planted. When we did not see his twenty-year-old car, we thought he was off to the village to sell his raspberries to the hotels. But when I got out of our car, I heard him chanting inside the old farmhouse. I approached carefully, not knowing whether he was praying alone or with others in the chapel he had created with his hands. I looked through the door. He was on his knees before the altar he had made from a grinding stone, and he was looking up at a simple forged cross. He sensed someone behind him and he slowly rose and came forward.

Père Grégoire was an eighty-year-old monk who lived alone. Over four years ago Jill had seen him at a small hotel, Les Herbes Blanches, where he was delivering his raspberries. She had asked him about the berries and been told that he needed help in picking his cherries (which had grown from trees he had planted from seed). She had persuaded our son Stephen to pick the crop, and when on the first day Stephen didn't know where to begin, Père Grégoire had told him, "Just follow the sun and pick where the sun shines."

Now, Père Grégoire kissed Jill, holding her hands warmly, and asked, "How is Stephen?" It had been two years since Stephen had been to see him and yet he remembered where Stephen was working. Père Grégoire wanted to know everything about us.

Inside his kitchen, we sat around a small table while Père Grégoire started to prepare the tea. He opened the refrigerator, took out tea and milk, filled a small pan with water, dipped two electric prongs in, and the tea was made. We ate his homemade bread. I looked out a window into his orchard, the field, and then the sky beyond. Then I studied the room and wondered what it would be like to live here alone, isolated, brutally cold in winter with the mistral blowing. But Jill and Père Grégoire were talking about the cherry trees, which this year had blossomed beautifully but bore no fruit. He rarely talked about himself except when we asked how he was feeling. He had never been sick a day in his life. "When the time does come for me to go, I look forward to this new experience with joy. I am sure the angels will be there to greet me. No one really goes to hell unless they want to."

The three of us looked at each other. Then Père Grégoire broke the silence: "I can give nothing to you, nothing at all, only my friendship." When we got up to say goodbye, he walked us to the car. We turned around and went up the hill, silently, realizing that Père Grégoire was right: friendship and love are all we can give.

There are those special moments of friendship that touch all of us. Among them is my memory of the eighty-year-old Sir Stephen Spender standing in our dusty driveway next to the olive grove. In his hand he was holding gently a plastic bag filled with water in which were three goldfish. He had brought them to us to put in our basin. Now, a year later, with those fish we have their offspring, still black but soon to turn gold.

Surrounded with all the beauty of Provence and of Switzerland, being with the friends who make up those scenes, we live a charmed life. But back in New York, that energizer of energizers, we are sometimes stimulated to such a high pitch that it is hard to wake up to the fact that after all what we are doing is neither great nor very important but just an ordinary job we really enjoy.

When we get so caught up in our world of the Chic Savages that we too are playing Snakes and Ladders, I try to remember the lesson I learned from becoming a Chevalier de la Légion d'Honneur. So bear with me for one more story.

It was two years ago when I went to the Quai d'Orsay in Paris to receive the decoration from Jean-Bernard Raimond, who was then the Minister for Foreign Affairs. As Jill and I arrived, the tall gold-framed doors of the palace were opened by a *huissier,* a gentleman-usher, with a long silver chain around his neck. In a deep voice he announced, "Monsieur and Madame Fairchild," as we walked into the eighteenth-century grand salon, which was filled with kilos of white orchids. I had a lump in my throat when I saw many of our friends, all looking so elegant, standing there waiting for us. Just then I realized the pants of my new navy Armani suit were unzipped. I remedied that quickly and went to greet my friends. I held Jill's hand nervously while Monsieur Raimond talked about what I had done for French fashion, and then I went up to him to receive my medal. The only problem was that as he pinned it on my breast he stuck me and I jumped—to everyone's amusement. I gave my speech, thanking the French government.

My head was swimming with pride after the ceremony and during a beautiful formal candlelight dinner given by our friend André Oliver and attended by Madame Claude Pompidou, widow of the former President of France, and by Madame Bernadette Chirac, wife of the then Prime Minister. And the next morning I was still feeling wonderful when I called up the housekeeper of the Ritz Hotel, where we were staying, and asked that the red ribbon of the Legion of Honor be sewn on the lapel of my suit. And I was wearing it proudly when I went out into the bright sunlight of the Place Vendôme. Standing there was a Texan who had just come out of the Ritz too. He asked me, "Aren't you an

American?" I told him I was. And then he said, "I just want to tell you you've got a red cleaning tag on your lapel. Can I take it off?"

I was too embarrassed and humbled to say anything except "Thank you." I dashed down the steps, hailed a taxi, jumped in, and thought to myself, "Fairchild, you will never make it as a Chic Savage."

INDEX